The Mourning After

The Mourning After

Help for Postabortion Syndrome

Terry Selby
with
Marc Bockmon

BAKER BOOK HOUSE
Grand Rapids, Michigan 49516

Library of Congress Cataloging-in-Publication Data

Selby, Terry.
    The mourning after: help for postabortion syndrome / Terry Selby with
Marc Bockmon.
            p.   cm.
    Includes bibliographical references.
    ISBN 0-8010-8310-9
    1. Abortion—Psychological aspects. 2. Abortion—Religious
aspects—Christianity. I. Bockmon, Marc, 1943– . II. Title.
RG734.S44   1990
618.8'8'019—dc20   90-39129
                                                                         CIP

Printed in the United States of America

To **God:**
Who gave me
my loving mother, Joyce;
and my loving father, Glenn;
who gave me life.

To **God:**
Who gave me
my loving wife, Judy;
who gave us our loving children
Kirstin and Nathan.

To **God:**
Who had this cycle all figured out.

Terry Selby
Bemidji, Minnesota

To **Marie:**
The love of my life,
bride of my youth,
mother of my children,
keeper of the faith,
wind beneath my wings,
wielder of the cruel red pen,
encourager, editor, friend.

Marc Bockmon
Mineola, Texas

Contents

Preface

What This Book Is *And* Is Not

The Mourning After is a book about helping and healing those who suffer from *postabortion syndrome (PAS)*. It is not, however, a book about abortion itself. It does not deal with the rightness or wrongness of abortion, but with reducing the trauma suffered by *some women* following an abortion.

The battle lines have been drawn on the abortion question for many years now, and prisoners are seldom taken by either side. I have my private opinions, of course. But those on either side looking for weaponry must look elsewhere, for I bring not ammunition but an ambulance to the conflict. I want to run up a flag of truce, carry the wounded off the field, and enable them to live full and productive lives.

In bringing help to hurting women, I realize that the language itself is a minefield that can trip the unwary. Depending on where you stand on the issue, the same entities may have very different names: anti-abortion/anti-choice; pro-abortion/pro-choice; anti-abortion/pro-life; or baby/fetus/product of conception/fetal tissue.

There are word watchers who would automatically turn off anyone who used the opposition's phraseology. Please do not do this. The problem of postabortion syndrome (PAS) is so severe and so many women are hurting that I would hate to see *either side* ignore the diagnostic guide-lines and treatments outlined in this book simply because I used the "other side's" terms. At one point, in fact, I considered alternating the terms and checking the number of uses with a computer to guarantee fairness. However, this made for some sentences that would choke a grammarian and often obscured the thought. Therefore, in speaking of what was aborted, I shall use *baby/POC* (POC for product of conception), hoping this will prove satisfactory to those on both sides of the issue. The only exceptions will be in case histories, where I shall use the terms the woman herself used in counseling.

Be warned ahead of time, however, that in actual counseling, women invariably say "baby." Not "fetus." Not "product of conception." Not "tissue." This is understandable, because *no woman mourns the loss of tissue*. If, in her mind, only a "bit of tissue" was removed in the abortion, she wouldn't be suffering from postabortion syndrome.

In my practice, I allow the patient to use whatever term she chooses. I don't impose my philosophy or my persuasions on her. She is not a pawn in a political game, but a patient seeking help. The intensity of the debate has kept many women with postabortion syndrome from seeking the counsel of family, friends, church, or clinicians—and I believe this is shameful.

As a clinical counselor, my task is to bind up wounds, heal hurts, and work to restore those who are hurting. As a Christian, I also see this helping process as part of a higher calling. But my personal beliefs are just that—personal. They color my life, but they do not color my practice and they do not alter the counseling techniques for PAS, which are based on generally accepted practice for treating post-traumatic stress disorder.

As far as postabortion syndrome is concerned, the issue is not what either political pole thinks or what I think or what the counseling industry as a whole thinks or what you think. The issue is what the postabortive woman thinks. Postabortion syndrome springs from her thoughts and her words and her concepts, not ours.

This, then, is a book about *help*, not a book about *blame*. It will deal not with what should or should not have been done, but with what *was* done. It will deal not with what women with postabortion syndrome should or should not feel, but with what they do feel—and with how they can come to grips with and work through the problem. This is a counselor's book, however, not a "do-it-yourself" book. I certainly hope that women suffering from PAS can read the book and be helped, especially by recognizing the symptoms and seeking professional, competent counsel. But my first purpose in writing is to equip and enable the clinical counselor to understand and treat postabortion syndrome.

I've found many clinical counselors (I mean those who offer *general counseling*, not those employed by abortion clinics themselves) are reluctant to be drawn into post-abortion counseling because it is such a "hot potato." I myself did not want to begin treating postabortion syndrome or to deal with the abortion issue for the same reason.

However, more and more hurting women came to me seeking treatment for emotional problems, marital dys-function, and chemical dependency that could be traced back to the abortion experience. I realized I had no choice but to explore this area. As I dealt with PAS using standard counseling techniques, the results were surprising: improvement was rapid and sometimes almost instanta-neous.

As of this writing, I have personally counseled more than one hundred women suffering from PAS. In addition, I have met with and compared case study notes with dozens of other clinicians who have, all told, treated well over a thousand patients suffering from PAS.

You may well ask, "Isn't a thousand case studies a rela-tively small sample?" Yes, it is, considering there have been over twenty million abortions in the United States since 1973. However, pollsters claim to be able to predict within three to four percentage points what two hundred and sixty million Americans think from less than sixteen hundred interviews. A thousand case studies from a twenty million base is a much higher sample than sixteen hundred interviews from a two-hundred-and-sixty million base.

What a thousand case studies tells us is that there is a significant problem and that the treatment outlined in this book is effective. What a thousand case studies *does not* tell us is the *size of the problem*. We have no way of knowing if PAS affects merely thousands or tens of thousands or hundreds of thousands of aborted women.[1]

PAS, for a variety of reasons, has been a private malady, much like post-Vietnam stress disorder once was. The sufferer has not felt she could discuss the issue. Mental-health professionals have shied away because of controversy and, in many instances, a preconceived idea that abortion is always a reasonably safe medical procedure with no lasting physical or psychological side effects. Based on the number we have found in our own practices, however, I suspect the number of women suffering from some form of postabortion syndrome may be quite large.

These women and those who care about them have suffered too long. Those of us who proudly proclaim ourselves to be counselors should cast aside our prejudices, preconceptions, and politics and help these women live happier, more meaningful lives. After all, that's what counseling is all about!

Terry Selby
Bemidji, Minnesota

1

Introduction
to Postabortion Syndrome

When the cause of the disease is not identified, the remedies will be of no avail. Manual Ayau

Someone you counsel or care about is hurting and experiencing emotional problems. These problems may include broken relationships, sexual performance problems, depression, anxiety, drug and/or alcohol abuse, or difficulties in bonding with children. If these symptoms began *after an abortion*, the cause may be postabortion syndrome (PAS). If so, this book has a message you need to hear and heed:

> There is hope.
> There is help.
> There is recovery.

But first, you have to learn something about the nature of the malady itself and how it begins.

"When the cause of the disease is not identified, the remedies will be of no avail." Manual Ayau, the man who said that, is an economist and statesman, not a medical doctor nor a clinical counselor. Yet the diagnostic requirement he spoke of applies to our fields as well. While we can treat symptoms while ignorant of the cause, the best we can expect from such treatment is symptomatic relief. Treatment of symptoms is preferable to no treatment at all, but it is not the best physical or psychological medicine.

The pain of appendicitis, for instance, may be treated with painkillers, but while this may effectively diminish discomfort, it has no effect on the root cause of the suffering. Pain is an alarm system that tells us something is wrong in our bodies or our minds. When we shut off the alarm without correcting the cause, the problem is likely to grow more severe. A patient with acute appendicitis who is treated with painkillers alone will almost certainly die!

In my practice, over the years many women have come to me with symptoms usually associated with post-traumatic stress disorder, such as depression, anxiety, behavioral problems, or chemical dependency. I have found ways to alleviate the symptoms, but all along I have felt the best treatment is to uncover the root cause of the problems. I knew from their histories that many of these women had had abortions, but quite frankly, I didn't attach much importance to that as a causal agent. Initially, my own mind-set was "Abortion can't be a problem because I haven't heard anyone say it's been a problem. Besides, this is *one* can of worms I don't want to open. It's too emotional."

Eventually, as I detail in chapter 2, I reached the point where I recognized PAS and developed an effective counseling technique for it. Nobody ever said counseling was an easy profession or for the faint of heart. If you're in the counseling profession, eventually you're going to have to deal with this syndrome. The best place to begin is by learning all about PAS you can.

What Is Postabortion Syndrome?

Postabortion syndrome (PAS) is a disorder that seems to be brought about by stress involved with the abortion itself and that, for one reason or another, the aborted woman is unable to process. This then would indicate that post-abortion syndrome is a type of post-traumatic stress disorder (PTSD). The symptoms of this disorder are succinctly given in the third edition (revised) of the American Psychiatric Association's DMS-III-R.[1] If you'd like a detailed definition, one is included in Appendix A, along with a detailed definition of postabortion syndrome itself (Appendix B).

Basically, post-traumatic stress disorder happens as a result of a particular stressful event, what mental-health professionals call a "stressor." In postabortion syndrome, the stressor is the abortion experience, that is, the intentional destruction of one's baby/POC. Some women who have undergone this procedure find it sufficiently traumatic to cause significant symptoms of reexperience and avoidance.[2]

The reexperience of the stress can take several forms. An aborted woman may have recurrent, intrusive recollections or dreams of the abortion or the child she might have had. She may have dreams or sudden panic feelings that the abortion is reoccurring.

Obviously, such phenomena are painful, and nobody likes pain. One way to avoid pain is to avoid anything that brings it back to mind—even memories of the event. PAS, therefore, has a strong element of denial. Unfortunately, shutting a mental door to keep out a stray thought is like shutting an actual door to keep out a stray cat—you shut out other things as well. Keeping the doors to our mind shut leads to avoidance, and avoidance in turn can lead to:

diminished interest in significant activities
feelings of detachment or estrangement from others

reduced capacity for feeling or expressing emotions
reduced communication and/or increased hostile inter-
    actions
depression

In the PAS patient, there may also be "associated symptoms" such as hyperalertness (an exaggerated startle reaction or explosive hostile outbursts), sleeplessness, memory
impairment, and concentration difficulties.

These symptoms may be intensified by exposure to
reminders of the abortion, such as contact with medical
personnel, pregnant mothers, nurseries, and so on. There
may also be feelings of guilt about the decision-making
process, or even for surviving when the baby/POC did
not, along with an inability to forgive herself.

The symptoms just described may be acute, beginning
within six months of the abortion; chronic, lasting longer
than six months; or delayed, beginning more than six
months after the event.

Postabortion Syndrome Springs from a Real Event

The woman suffering from postabortion syndrome may
feel guilt at what she has done. However, there is no evidence that guilt itself triggers PAS. Rather, the suffer is
reacting to a real event in her life. The *DMS III*, referring to
post-traumatic stress disorder, cites a classic case of a
woman who was raped in an elevator and now breaks out
in a cold sweat every time she enters one. In the same way,
a PAS woman may strongly react to any reminder of an
event that she perceived as traumatic.

The root cause of postabortion syndrome seems to be
stress involved with the abortion itself, though a woman's
personal belief system may add to the stress. In classic
DMS III diagnostic terms, stressors are objects or events
that create a startle reaction. In the case of PAS, these reactions could come from a variety of sources—the "vacuum
cleaner" sound of the aspirator in the abortion clinic, unex-

pected pain, the clinical detachment of the clinic staff, or the sight of the aborted baby/POC. True, the reaction may be mitigated and enhanced by the woman's beliefs and values—but that is a subsequent reaction, an *interpretation* of the stress she experienced.

Because PAS is rooted in the abortion experience itself, the type of abortion plays a role in the development of PAS symptoms, as does the stage of pregnancy at which the abortion is done.

If it is an "early on" abortion, early enough to carry the euphemism "menstrual extraction," then the pain may not be severe, and stress may be minimal. The more advanced the pregnancy, however, the greater the trauma. For one thing, a symbiotic relationship has begun to develop between the woman and the baby/POC. Her body is changing. Her menstrual periods have ceased, and hormones are flowing through her system. She may have sensed a thickening and enlarging of the waist and breasts or have felt movement in her womb. The more changes that occur in her body, the more likely she is to feel a sense of loss—and therefore to develop PAS.

The more advanced pregnancy also requires a more advanced medical procedure and inherently more pain. A later-term abortion that requires a saline injection is often much more difficult to mentally process. If a woman has to go to a hospital and go through birth pains to deliver a perfectly formed twenty-two week old dead, red baby/POC (see Appendix C for a description of the five leading abortion procedures), she may not be able to process the ensuing stress. In cases where there has been a great deal of pain and/or trauma, PAS may set in almost immediately.

The Denial Factor

Studies indicate that the pain and stress of an abortion may be the root cause of postabortion syndrome and the greater the stress, the greater the likelihood of PAS devel-

oping. Stress, however, is not the only contributing factor.
Guilt over the procedure, grief over the perceived loss, and
a feeling of victimization are also common in the PAS sufferer. Even more important, however, is her *inability to process* that trauma and its accompanying feelings because of
denial and a tendency to repress her thoughts or feelings
about this event.

Now a certain amount of denial is normal and even
healthy. People avoid thinking about certain traumatic
events and emotions in order to alleviate physical or psychological pain. We find denial at work after auto acci-
dents, fire, or wartime experiences. In these cases, denial
enables us to postpone processing what has happened
until the crisis is over. Then, with the support of family,
friends and society, we can work through our pain and
grief.

In the case of PAS, however, the woman has no place to
process her trauma. She has had a real, painful, perhaps
frightening experience—and she can't talk about it. There
is almost no social support for women who find abortion a
stressful experience, because almost every group involved
with abortion has its own set of agendas.

Pro-life/anti-choice groups rarely reach out to comfort
and console aborted women who experience pain or grief.
Those in this group are likely to feel, "You murdered your
baby; how did you expect to feel?" Pro-abortion/pro-
choice groups tend to treat the feelings as an embarrassment that shouldn't be happening: "It's your body, and it
was your decision. It was just a piece of tissue, and you
shouldn't feel bad." Both groups tend to neglect or ignore
the aborted woman herself. Counselors typically don't
want to touch this "controversial" issue. And families and
friends may be so close to the event that they cannot be
supportive or have been shut out from the event and don't
even know it occurred.

Some aborted women, therefore, continue in denial
rather than working through their pain, guilt, and grief.
This may involve denying certain feelings or beliefs about

abortion, repressing memories of certain events—or even denying that the abortion took place at all.[3]

Therefore, it's the *combination* of an acute experience of abortion trauma, guilt, and having no forum to process this real experience that typically leads to PAS.

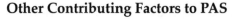

Other Contributing Factors to PAS

There are indications that PAS may be somewhat age sensitive. That is, the younger the woman is at the time of the abortion, the more likely she is to develop PAS. A sixteen year-old will have a very different reaction to an abortion than a twenty-five-year-old, if for no other reason than the fact that the person has less experience in processing trauma, denial, and pain.[4] It is the nature of adolescence to be self-centered and independent, as well as family-centered and dependent. The law permits teenagers to make an adult decision on abortion without having to seek family or adult counsel, regardless of their level of maturity. Whatever the value judgment, a decision to abort means that life, or potential life, is gone forever. The decision not to abort means that life, or potential life, is a lifetime responsibility. This is clearly an adult decision.

Am I saying that a college-educated career woman of thirty-five who is a member of the National Organization of Women and a contributor to Planned Parenthood is less likely to have a problem than a girl of sixteen? Based on our own research, she has statistically better odds, perhaps because her defense mechanisms are more developed, and she has placed herself in a social situation that supports her decision and continues to reinforce it.

An alcoholic who stays in the bar has little trouble suppressing his negative feelings about his drinking. He is in a social situation where it is understood, accepted, and even encouraged. He gets lots of positive reinforcement. However, if he has been picked up three times for driving while intoxicated and has lost his job, it becomes harder for him to deny he has a problem. (This is not to compare the abortion industry with the mixed drink industry, merely a way of pointing out that positive reinforcement can be expected from the provider of any service.)

Language is also an aid in maintaining denial. Therefore, in any conflict, the group that defines the language has the high ground. In Vietnam, objectives weren't *destroyed*, they were *neutralized*. General Chuck Yeager said that no test pilots were *killed*, they *augured in*. "Neutralized" or "augured in" doesn't sound as harsh as more traditional language meaning the same thing. The language helps maintain denial. By the same token, those opposed to private ownership of firearms call their movement "handgun control." That's a pretty effective piece of namesmanship—who could be for handguns *out of* control? The same is true of the legal organization who named itself "American Civil Liberties Union"—it was a bit of namesmanship that makes any opposition look like they're *against* American civil liberties! Or what about the organization formerly called the "Moral Majority?" If you were against anything they stood for, the name implied you were neither moral nor in the majority!

In the abortion battle, proponents of legal abortion tend to avoid the term *pro-abortion* and speak instead of *pro-choice*. They do not say their opponents are *anti-abortion*, but *anti-choice*. The implication is powerful, for who could be against choice? On the other hand, opponents of legal abortion choose different language. They do not consider themselves so much as *anti-choice* but as *pro-life*. (Who could be against life?)

The choice of language is important because words bring up certain images in our minds. *Baby* has one mental image, *embryo* another, *fetus* another and *product of conception* or *fetal tissue* yet another. The use of euphemistic language helps the woman maintain denial through the abortion and often beyond. A woman might hesitate to abort a "baby" because of her mental image of the word. She would be somewhat less hesitant to abort a "product of conception" or "fetal tissue" because these are impersonal terms, devoid of traditional mothering images.

The deliberate use of euphemistic or clinical language to refer to an abortion has advanced so far that a woman who has missed one period is sometimes told she doesn't need an abortion at all to protect herself from pregnancy—a *menstrual extraction* can solve any potential problem.

By calling an abortion a menstrual extraction, the woman who undergoes the procedure can tell herself she isn't having an abortion because she wasn't *sure* she was pregnant. However, unless she routinely has menstrual extractions, deep inside she realizes she did something different and that there was a reason for choosing abortion this time.

However, where the desire to believe is strong, language is a nuance, a subtlety, a device to help build or maintain denial. Language, properly used during "the procedure," helps the woman believe what she wants to believe. The problem is that denial based on language alone doesn't last.

I worked with a PAS patient who had a menstrual extraction. Since I never attempt to impose my definitions or values on a client, I asked her what she thought a "menstrual extraction" was. She said, "It's an abortion. I knew I was pregnant when I had it done. My breasts were thickening, I was retaining water, and I felt a difference in my body. It was early in my pregnancy, and the doctor said I didn't test positive, but to be 'on the safe side' they would do a menstrual extraction."

The language let her off the hook momentarily, because the physician taught her to call what *she knew* to be an abortion something else. Her denial mechanism was operating at peak efficiency as she left the doctor's office. The denial wasn't strong enough to keep postabortion syndrome from developing, but it did postpone its arrival until much later.

Another patient shared an event that shows just how effective denial can be for a short time. She went into an abortion clinic for counseling on Tuesday. She was told she had a "product of conception" in her "conception vessel," a "mass of tissue no different than any other tissue," but it would be best to remove .it. She bought into that and believed that, so she scheduled the abortion for Thursday. Yet that afternoon, as she ran to class, she instinctively held her stomach so she "wouldn't hurt the baby!" She had the abortion two days later, and I saw her as a PAS patient two years afterward.

How Many Women Suffer from Postabortion Syndrome?

There are no statistics that would give us a handle on just how many women may have PAS. One reason is that the issue of abortion is so emotional and political. The perception of a hostile attitude by pro- and anti- forces, plus a natural shyness about discussing a painful, private matter, have kept many of these women silent, and there are no hard numbers. As the Surgeon General pointed out, the fact that many women who have had abortions deny it raises further concern about the accuracy of any numbers that are available.

The shortage of numbers, while explainable, handicaps our efforts to draw attention to the seriousness of the problem. Our nation is very numbers-conscious, and unless we hear that "three in ten" or "two in five" or "one in twenty" suffer from a malady, we tend to attach little importance to it. To my mind, this is an unfortunate trend, because whether a number is large or small, each digit represents an individual sufferer. This trend certainly should be shunned by clinicians, whose entire training is focused on solving the problems of people one at a time.

Another reason PAS numbers are difficult to amass is that patients tend to suppress the cause of their difficulties. Clinicians can be misled because the symptoms are similar to other types of trauma. Also, since it is possible to obtain *some symptomatic relief* without arriving at a complete diagnosis, some clinicians stop short of asking the necessary diagnostic questions when they suspect the root cause may be abortion trauma. Abortion is, quite simply, too intense for some clinicians to handle—and many have their own value judgments about how the woman should or should not feel.

It may be difficult to find hard numbers on postabortion syndrome for the same reason that it was and is difficult to find hard numbers on those suffering from post-Vietnam stress disorder. The Vietnam vet, like the aborted woman, found himself caught in a crossfire between two opposing groups. When returning combat vets began having problems with substance abuse, establishing careers and building lasting relationships, they didn't want to relate these problems to the war, and neither did mental health professionals. The vets' experiences became a very private thing that only came out under intense counseling or, occasionally, among peers.

There are many other parallels between Vietnam vets and postaborted women. Both events were highly politicized, with one group telling them they had done the right thing and another group telling them they were murderers and should suffer for it.

The veterans were unable to obtain help until they themselves organized and began demanding treatment. It was only then that those of us in the mental-health sector woke up and began looking at the Vietnam experience as a *possible cause* of *some of the emotional problems* that were being experienced by *some veterans*. Even then, because of the negative political pressure, it took a long time for the full extent of the problem to be recognized. The same thing is probably true of postabortion syndrome. Neither pro-abortion/pro-choice or anti-abortion/anti-choice groups want to talk about it. Therefore, these women tend to keep their hurt to themselves, and their counselors don't ask questions about it because (1) they feel it isn't a problem and (2) they aren't sure how to cope with the answers.

We finally became aware of the scope of post-Vietnam stress disorder after veteran support groups forced us as citizens and clinicians to face the problem with them. It is likely we won't fully realize the full extent and severity of postabortion syndrome until PAS support groups make us face this issue as well. So far, there are no well established groups.[5]

However, whether there is a large number or a small number is rather meaningless if one of those numbers represents someone you are counseling. This book is designed to help you help that person.

Once again, I am not saying that *all* women who have an abortion suffer postabortion syndrome. I am not even saying that *most* women who have an abortion suffer from postabortion syndrome. I am saying that *some women who have abortions suffer from postabortion syndrome.* This book is designed to help those women, whether they number in the thousands, tens of thousands, hundreds of thousands, or millions.

Factors *Not* at the Root of Postabortion Syndrome

Based on my own clinical studies, as well as others that I have reviewed, postabortion syndrome *does not seem to be related to:*

1. *Length of time since the abortion.* I treated one fifty-five year old woman who was suffering postabortion syndrome as a result of an abortion she had undergone *thirty-five years* earlier. A counselor who read an early draft of this book asked if abortion procedures decades ago were more traumatic than current ones. Perhaps, but I think not. Actress Gloria Swanson, in her eighties, was still despondent and depressed over an abortion she had fifty-five years earlier. Another actress, Shelley Winters, in discussing her abortions has been quoted as saying, "I would give up everything—my money, my Academy Award, my career—if only I could have those children now."

2. *Marital status.* Whether or not a woman was married at the time of the abortion doesn't seem relevant to

the onset of postabortion syndrome. In my practice, I have treated women who were:

> unmarried when aborted and unmarried at the time of counseling
>
> unmarried when aborted and married at the time of counseling
>
> married when aborted and unmarried at the time of counseling
>
> married when aborted and married at the time of counseling

3. *Family size.* Family size, previous pregnancies, or later ones, seem to have no effect in the onset of postabortion syndrome. We have found women with postabortion syndrome who:

> have no children
>
> have children born *prior to* the abortion
>
> have children born *subsequent to* the abortion
>
> have children born *prior to* and *subsequent to* the abortion

4. *Religious affiliation.* This also seems to have little effect on the onset of PAS. Frankly, at first I found this surprising, because my initial assumption was that external guilt was the primary causal agent, and therefore that close affiliation with a church that opposes abortion would increase the chance of PAS. However, in my counseling I have encountered PAS women who:

> are nominally Christian
>
> are evangelically Christian
>
> are Jewish
>
> follow Indian tribal religion
>
> have no religious background

However, the woman's *personal convictions*—especially her belief about the nature and meaning of the abortion, *does* play a role in development of PAS.

Women who *truly believe* (not just talk themselves into believing) that they are aborting only "tissue" or a "mass of cells" do not develop PAS.

5. *External guilt.* A woman suffering from PAS feels not only grief but guilt. This guilt rarely comes from *without*, it invariably comes from *within*. The opinions of family, friends or pro-life/anti-choice groups do not seem to have an effect in the development of postabortion syndrome. However, once a woman is suffering from PAS, external guilt stimuli such as seeing a anti-abortion/anti-choice ad, seeing children the age hers might have been, and so on can exacerbate the condition. This occurs primarily when new data, such as photos of unborn babies/POCs are introduced.

Considerations in Treating PAS

To bring relief to the PAS sufferer, the clinician must initially be concerned with four aspects of PAS: the actual experience of the abortion, unresolved grief, denial, and lifestyle denial.

1. *The abortion experience.* A woman may have the coping skills to handle one or more facets of the abortion experience, but the totality of the experience may be too much for her to handle. A woman must process the social context of the abortion, the preabortion interview, the interaction with nurses and doctor, the feeling of vulnerability, the sounds of the equipment, the discomfort or pain as instruments are inserted and, in a latter-term abortion, the actual delivery of a dead baby/POC.

We are at our best in processing events *similar* to events we've experienced before. This allows us to draw on past experience. When a woman undergoes an abortion, particularly a first abortion, she has nothing within her experience bank to draw on for support. Also, she has little or no societal support, as she would have if she had a miscarriage or lost a full-term infant. When the number of stressors outside her experience grow beyond her capacity, PAS is the likely result.

2. *Unresolved grief.* If the abortion experience is the basic causal event of PAS, then PAS in essence is a matter of unresolved grief over that event. Helping a PAS woman recover, therefore, is a matter of helping her face and work through her grief.

   This may fly in the face of many preconceived notions about how a woman should or should not feel after an abortion. But once again, I am not talking about the *clinicians* perception of what the postabortive woman *should feel*, but about what she actually feels. Simply put, if a woman is experiencing unresolved grief as the result of an abortion, then she has postabortion syndrome. It can be mild, moderate, chronic, or acute-but the diagnosis is the same. And the treatment must involve helping her process that grief.

3. *Denial.* The third aspect of PAS a clinician must deal with is denial of the facts and feelings associated with the event. This may include denial of the pain, of the memory, of the clinic, of the abortion room, of the procedure, and of her feelings along the way. (The denial may extend to the clinician as well, he or she may deny that abortion can have anything to do with a patient's problems.)

   This denial can be difficult to break. A counselor who asks "Do you grieve the loss of a pregnancy through abortion?" is almost certain to get a negative answer. It may be true that the woman is not grieving. However, it is also possible that denial is at work. For this reason, a large part of treating PAS is detecting or breaking denial. I will cover this in detail in a later chapter.

4. *Lifestyle of denial.* Denial can lead to a lifestyle of denial. Possible results of such a lifestyle include:

> broken or dysfunctional relationships
> sexual performance problems
> depression
> anxiety
> drug and/or alcohol abuse
> poor parent-child bonding

Any of these, therefore, can be considered possible symptoms of PAS. A comprehensive list of symptoms can be found in Appendix B.

PAS: The Bottom Line to Chapter One

If the symptoms of trauma an aborted woman is experiencing began after an abortion, you, as a counselor, have a responsibility to ask about that event in her life. If she has trouble recalling the event or telling about it, she may be suffering from postabortion syndrome. Also, if she obviously feels grief and has not resolved that grief, then you will need to guide her through those steps.

So far, I have only touched on the extent and the symptoms of the problem. I will cover all these subjects in more detail as I proceed. It is important that we convey to all women (and some men!) who are suffering from postabortion syndrome:

> There is help.
> There is hope.
> There is recovery.

2

My First Encounters with PAS

One of the reasons governments and industries tend to lag in acknowledging problems is the issue of culpability. If an organization admits it did something that damaged someone, then it is legally responsible for the damage. That's why cigarette companies continue to claim there is insufficient proof that smoking is a causal agent for lung cancer, emphysema, heart disease and a host of other maladies. The manufacturers of Agent Orange denied the chemical's harmful effects for the same reason. Asbestos manufacturers still deny the harmful effects of asbestos. The makers of a highly advertised flea and tick killer for pets denied any problem with their initial release of the product long after people began writing to complain of dead dogs. Today, some car companies are protesting evidence that their cars tend to turn over or accelerate without warning for the same reason. Legally speaking, it's bad legal practice to admit you did something that injured someone.

The abortion industry performs approximately 1.8 million abortions a year. At an average cost of $400 each, this represents gross sales of $720,000,000 a year—roughly two million dollars a day. It is reasonable to assume the industry would be as reticent as, say, the chemical, asbestos, tobacco, and automobile businesses to admit to a potentially expensive legal problem.

There is nothing wrong with being a big, profitable business, but as the late Dr. Lawrence J. Peter said in his classic business book, *The Peter Principle*, "The first rule of business is that the hierarchy must be preserved." The huge demand for abortion service has made the abortion industry big business in America. Quite naturally, those who draw their livelihood from this business would like to see the hierarchy preserved.

This is not to imply that those within the abortion industry would hide facts to protect the bottom line. But it would be somewhat unreasonable for us to expect that they would be any more likely to jump to a detrimental conclusion than the tobacco and car companies have. Negative feedback from injured clients is unlikely to be encouraged, much less advertised—and the injured parties are unlikely to protest. Few people would be embarrassed to admit they developed cancer from smoking or were injured by a defective automobile. But many women are embarrassed to admit they have had an abortion, regardless of the problems they suffer later.

Considering the reluctance of many women to discuss their postabortion problems, the reluctance of clinicians to get involved in "new maladies," and the tremendous political and fiscal power of the abortion industry, it is not surprising we are just beginning to hear about PAS. However, just as a veritable avalanche of patients with post-Vietnam stress disorder began to pour into counseling offices after vets with the problem realized they were not alone, we can expect to find more PAS sufferers as the symptoms, causes, and treatment for PAS become more widely known.

In the meantime, however, most of us in the mental health field are a conventional lot. We like precedence and tradition and well-thought-out, well-proven techniques and treatments. We do not tend to be on the "leading edge" of what's happening. We are trained to listen, think, wait, and analyze.

On the whole, this is good. After all, emotional problems are nothing new, and one has to have valid reasons for forsaking the tried and true for something that is new and different. But the down side of our conservatism is that we often fail to be on the forefront of what happens when new stressors are introduced. Postabortion syndrome, like post-Vietnam stress disorder, didn't begin to get our attention until aborted women began to come out of their private hells and to share their agonies. Even then, we looked for *other causes*. In fact, so few have spoken up that some counselors, pastors, clinicians, psychiatrists, and naturally the industry itself, still deny the possibility of postabortion syndrome.

My First PAS Patient: Betty

Sherlock Holmes, the great fictional detective, said, "When you have eliminated the impossible, whatever else remains, however improbable, must be the truth." The process of elimination first led me to suspect that abortion *might* be a contributing cause to emotional distress in 1983. But had it not been for the courage and cooperation of a woman I'll call Betty,[1] my clinic might still be treating the symptoms instead of the malady.

Betty was thirty-one, and she, too, was a clinical counselor. On the surface, she appeared to have it all together. She was active in feminist causes, a fifteen-year contributor to Planned Parenthood, and a leader in her local National Organization of Women (NOW) chapter. She and her second husband had three normal, healthy children.

Betty first came to see me for severe marital problems. Over a period of a year, we went through a very intense series of treatments that identified several problems, including a history of chemical dependency which had begun when she was fifteen. Her father had died of a wasting, lingering disease, and his death had been more than Betty felt she could handle alone. She had turned to alcohol and sexual promiscuity to dull the emotional pain she was feeling. Later she had added street drugs to her chemical regimen.

Reliving the loss of her father in our sessions and being allowed to grieve for him opened up some old, festering wounds and allowed a certain amount of healing to take place. Yet, it was obvious to both of us that her problems involved something more, something deeper, something neither she nor I had faced before.

One afternoon after a session, I stopped her at the door and asked, "Betty, is there anything else that might be a primary cause that you haven't told me about?"

She paused, then said, "Well, I've had an abortion, but that's not a problem."

I said, "I don't know if it'll do any good or not, but why don't we talk about that next session and see?"

At the next session, we did delve into the abortion, and the experience was like lancing a boil. Anguish and hurt and guilt gushed out, and a sense of relief followed.

Betty's abortion had taken place when she was sixteen. Her mother was still trying to deal with the loss of her husband and raise three daughters. Betty didn't feel she could add this weight to the burden her mother carried. Without telling anyone, she went to the local family planning office and asked for advice. This was in 1971, two years before the Supreme Court ruled abortion legal, but they counseled Betty to have an abortion anyway. They told her the laws were more lax in another state and that they were flying a group of teenage girls there the following day to have abortions together. The counselor patted Betty's hand and said, "You'll all be home before dark, and no one will ever know! You don't even have to tell your mother."

So Betty went to a more liberal state and had a vacuum-aspiration abortion. She came home and bled for several days, easing the physical and psychological pain by increasing her intake of alcohol. She never told anyone about the abortion.

Betty's second abortion had occurred when she was

nineteen. She was in college then and she and her boyfriend had consumed prodigious quantities of alcohol and marijuana daily. Soon they were married, and almost immediately she got pregnant. He wasn't ready for parenthood and insisted she have an abortion. He took her to an abortion clinic and waited outside while they aborted the fourteen week old baby/POC. When it was over, they went back to their apartment and smoked pot all weekend.

In recounting the story, Betty told me, "I wanted this baby but my husband didn't. Because I loved him, I committed what I thought was the ultimate act of sacrifice for him but he just didn't think it was any big deal. I was disgusted with him and with myself." By this time, Betty had already abandoned her mother and sisters. Within a year she abandoned her husband (an all-too-common result of an abortion, based on my counseling experience) and then abandoned herself. Her drug use escalated to the addiction level, and she stopped taking care of herself.

Betty was an interesting case because she was both counselor and counseled and was able to apply her professional insight to her own case history. She said, "I know from my own training that it's easy to remain obsessed when you feel you've made the ultimate sacrifice. It's hard to realize the ultimate sacrifice wasn't enough.

"I was afraid I could never have another child after that. I was afraid I'd blown it permanently and that God would punish me for what I did to my babies."

As I mentioned before, in counseling, I call the baby/POC whatever the patient calls it. If she calls it a "fetus," then it's a fetus. If she calls it a "product of conception," then that's what it is. When Betty would say "baby," there would be an immediate emotional reaction and she would quickly attempt to cover it up by clearing her throat or by moving quickly past the word. I asked her why and she said, "I cover up because I feel remorse whenever I say 'baby' or 'abortion.' It's just like the feeling I have when I talk about my father and his death . . . just as deep."

She averted her eyes from mine and flicked an invisible piece of lint from her skirt. "You know, when Dad died, I knew I should grieve. It was expected of me, people encouraged it. Yet this feeling is just as deep and I know I shouldn't grieve. Everyone tells me it's okay . . . that I shouldn't feel bad."

I suddenly realized we were dealing with a genuine grieving process here—one that had been thwarted for a decade. I said to her, "Betty, I'm not sure about this, but I want to make the assumption that the grief you're feeling now over this . . . baby is no more or less important than that you feel over your father. So we're going to proceed with the notion that you're stuck here emotionally, just as you were originally stuck emotionally with your father's death. When you say 'fetus' or 'product of conception,' you don't have a grieving reaction, but you do when you say 'baby,' so let's use that term."

"It hurts to say 'baby,'" she said. "But it feels right. I don't like the feeling, but it's right."

She continued her story and told about meeting her current husband. It was a relationship that began when they became "drinking buddies" and continued through an alcoholic courtship and marriage. Shortly after she married, she became pregnant a third time, and there was never any thought of not carrying the baby to term. As she told me about that pregnancy, she began sobbing. "I went through the pregnancy this time but I couldn't deny what I had done to my first two children."

After the tears subsided somewhat, I asked Betty to share what she could remember about her first abortion at age sixteen. I was amazed at the sharp, clear memory of *pain*. As Betty began to tell me about it, she closed her eyes and cried and writhed in agony and moaned and even screamed at the recollection. She was sixteen years old, in a strange place and a strange city, and medical instruments were being stuck into her uterus.

She said, "They strapped my legs in stirrups, and a sturdy nurse held my shoulders down. I didn't want to be there, but I felt I had no choice. I was surprised that the doctor was so rough, that it hurt so much. The pain was immense as he inserted the instruments and then the wand of the vacuum thing [aspirator] into me."

She paused, wept quietly for a moment, and added, "Then they sucked my baby out." Betty had been afraid and hadn't wanted to go through the experience of reliving the abortion, but she didn't see any other way out. As she relived the trauma of this real experience, the pain subsided to a manageable level and we went on to deal with the second abortion.

Thanks to Betty, I began to realize that PAS is caused by a real event—by the trauma and pain of the abortion itself. Since then, other women have shared similar stories, but had I counseled with them first, I might not have seen the connection, because few are as articulate as Betty was. Many women just cry and moan and can't put into words their thoughts and feelings. Because of Betty's unique training, she could see her event as both patient and clinician. She could talk her way through what were, for her anyway, horrible experiences.

Case History: Sue Ellen

Shortly after Betty's breakthrough, I began counseling another patient with an abortion in her background. Sue Ellen had been a nineteen-year-old college sophomore living with her boyfriend, when she became pregnant. Because she felt a pregnancy would cause problems at home, at school, and with her relationship, she had a vacuum aspiration abortion at fourteen weeks.

Three years later, when she was nearly twenty-three years old, Sue Ellen came into my offices for counseling. At this point, she felt unable to function sexually. She experienced pain in her vagina (phantom vaginal pain is commonly experienced by PAS women) and stomach during intercourse and felt this had led to the breakup of the relationship with the live-in lover who had impregnated her.

Since the breakup with her live-in, Sue Ellen had found herself unable to maintain a close relationship with any man. In fact, she had become quite fearful of developing an intimate relationship because she knew that when she was sexually aroused she would begin to feel the pain again.

The abortion also affected her relationship with her family. She and her mother had always been close and had shared everything. Now she felt uncomfortable around her mother, especially since her mother was always suggesting that she get married and raise a family. Since Sue Ellen couldn't enjoy sex, marriage seemed out of the picture for her, so she avoided the painful reminders by avoiding her mother.

To further complicate matters, a close friend had her first child about the time Sue Ellen would have delivered had she gone full term. The friend was in that early maternal stage where she constantly cooed to the baby and cuddled it, and she wanted Sue Ellen to share this experience with her. She was always handing the baby to her friend and became concerned when Sue Ellen stiffened and didn't want to take it. This experience put a lot of strain on Sue Ellen and she soon began avoiding her friend.

Now all Sue Ellen's primary relationships were in turmoil. Her boyfriend was gone, and she was unable to establish a relationship with anyone else. She felt alienated from her mother and her best friend. She had once been active in church, but now she felt like a phony and dropped out. Her grades in college dropped dramatically, and she finally quit school.

Sue Ellen's sense of self-worth underwent a radical change also. She had a poor perception of her body and couldn't stand to see herself in the mirror. She developed an eating disorder and wouldn't eat for days on end.

She decided the only way to get on with her life was to "pull herself together," so she enrolled in college and went to see her college counselor about the things that were happening in her life. As Sue Ellen related her post abortion feelings, the counselor became quite brisk and said, "I don't see that as part of the problem. Why should it be? Abortion is a safe, proven medical procedure."

The counselor more or less summed up her advice by saying, "The bottom line is that you *did* have an abortion and maybe it wasn't the best thing in the world *for you*, but it was your choice and it's behind you now. Let's get you up in the morning by eight o'clock and let's get you through your day and do some confirming activities. Go out and have a good time and just be yourself."

In my opinion, that counselor was being irresponsible, because she was doing an overlay of her own attitude about abortion onto her patient. She had determined that Sue Ellen shouldn't be feeling pain as a result of the abortion and therefore chose to ignore it as a possible cause for Sue Ellen's problems. If Sue Ellen had been an alcoholic and the counselor had been a family member, we would have classified her as an "enabler," because she enabled her to continue the process of denial.

If the counselor had already decided Sue Ellen's mother was a shrew and the mother had died, would she have counseled her that grieving was unnecessary? I think not. Yet that counselor had decided the loss of the baby/POC wasn't worth grieving about and on that basis had told Sue Ellen to put the matter behind her, get up early, and have a nice day.

Sue Ellen didn't feel she had aborted a *mass of tissue*. She felt she had aborted a *baby*. She felt bad about it, and the only person she had confided in had told her to buck up and have a nice day. She didn't want to get up early, and she never had a nice day because there was unresolved emotion in her life. Thinking happy thoughts until she turned blue wouldn't handle the problem of unresolved trauma.

When Sue Ellen told the counselor about the physical side of her problem, she was assured the symptoms had nothing to do with the emotional problem. The counselor suggested she have a complete physical to determine the cause of the stomach and vaginal pain.

Sue Ellen went to her family doctor, and after he had run every test he knew, she went into the hospital for X-rays, a gynecological workup, and a CAT scan. Her physicians found nothing organically wrong with her, and they weren't privy to the information she had given her counselor. They did not know the cause of the malady, so they did the next best thing: they treated the pain with painkillers.

Sue Ellen took her medication, she got up early, and she went back to school. But she couldn't concentrate, and she couldn't sleep. When she closed her eyes or let her mind drift, she saw babies that were broken and torn to pieces. This preoccupation continued and to alleviate her nightmares and depression, she turned first to alcohol, then to street drugs.

Postabortion syndrome, like blood poisoning, had spread throughout Sue Ellen's body. Treating *part* of her, whether emotionally or physically, had minimal result. It did little good to provide something to quiet her stomach, because the stomach pain was a symptom and not a cause. For the same reason, telling her to think positive thoughts did little good. It didn't even help for her to hear in church that she was forgiven, because she had not forgiven herself, or for her family to tell her she was loved and accepted, because she did not love or accept herself. She heard the words of love, but she thought, "You're saying that because *you don't know what I know.*" When I first saw Sue Ellen, I realized I had to treat the whole person. I would have to get to the *cause of the problem* for the remedy to be of avail. In many cases, clinical counselors will immediately try for symptom relief, but in this case I sensed that treating the clinical depression without finding the root cause would be harmful and not helpful. Besides, since she had already been down that road, I sensed that merely treating the symptoms would be ill-advised at best and little more than "professional enabling" at worse.

In counseling, Sue Ellen revealed that her abdominal and vaginal pain had appeared shortly after the abortion and had continued long after any medical reason for it to exist. The position she had assumed for the abortion was similar to the position she assumed for intercourse. Penetration reminded her of the instruments and the pain that followed.

"Oh," you say, "then the pain wasn't real." No, the pain *was real*—it was *very real*. It just had no physical basis. When a soldier has a leg amputated and wakes up with pain in that foot, it is phantom pain, but it is pain nevertheless.

In treating Sue Ellen, I was able to help her come to terms with her past and begin the process of healing. As she relieved herself of the burden of unresolved grief and personal guilt, the physical and the psychological pain diminished. She disclosed the abortion to her family and her family relationships were rebuilt. She overcame her chemical dependency, her grades improved, and she again became a part of her family's religious life. She has come to terms with the past and left the emotion of the memories there while retaining the memories themselves. Her PAS behind her, Sue Ellen has now married and is optimistic about the future. And I am grateful to her for what she taught me about PAS.

Case History: Brenda

Brenda was undergoing counseling for chemical dependency and had an abortion in her past. I sensed that this was a problem for her. However, her denial was strong, and she had difficulty opening up in one-on-one counseling sessions, so I suggested she join a therapy group.

Brenda wasn't as articulate as Betty or Sue Ellen and had always been shy about discussing her problem. However, one night she seemed to want to communicate with the group, and I suggested she openly share her feelings with us.

"I keep seeing broken babies in my head," she said. "I'm obsessed and horrified by it. How can I be sitting here talking to you when pictures of broken babies are flashing in my head? I have to stay here and act socially appropriate, but I'm having a hard time. I feel crazy when this is happening to me. I feel schizophrenic. Still, I don't feel I can talk about it."

In this group, I had discussed psychodrama before, pointing out that it is sometimes useful in drawing out the innermost feelings of those who have trouble expressing them. Now I explained, "Psychodrama is a clinical process that allows a person to relive a past event in the here and now. You do this by recalling the past in detail and acting out your thoughts without explaining them."

I turned to Brenda and said, "Brenda, let's do a little psychodrama. Let yourself act this out and see what happens. Let yourself be the baby a moment and *show* us what's happening to you!"

She got down out of her chair and lay on the floor. None of us was certain what she was going to do, but in a moment it became crystal clear. She curled into a fetal position, pulling back and struggling as an imaginary aspirator came near her. She jerked her feet up repeatedly as she tried to get away from the deadly vacuum. She *was* that baby. We watched for fifteen minutes as Brenda squirmed and fought and backed away and kicked. She spoke no words, just groaned and moaned. The whole group was mesmerized. Finally, the tube "got" her, and we watched as she scooted toward it. And as the abortion experience ended, she emitted a primeval wail that sent chills down spines. The emotional pain in that sound was unbelievable.

Brenda's grieving was totally different than Betty's: instead of describing her feelings, she merely made noises. Later, when the experience ended, she told us what was happening in her mind. She said she felt that the tube was going to get her and she didn't want to die, that she had to fight for her life. She also said that the experience was as real (and as exhausting) as if she had been fighting for her life for fifteen minutes against ten assassins. It was that real for her.

Brenda had gone into her own personal hell and faced

what she thought had happened during her abortion. Somehow, identifying with her baby/POC made the memory of the abortion bearable. Recovery seems to require a facing of the denied or suppressed memory and even a bonding with the "victim" of the abortion. While those who hold that life begins at birth will naturally take exception to the term *victim*, we must remember, once again that we are proceeding from the *perspective of the postaborted woman* and how she views the willful, forceful removal of the product of conception from her womb. This is not surprising when you consider that mothers-to-be who carry to full term often begin to identify with the baby early on. Women with postabortion syndrome seem to have a deep emotional need to bond with the baby, even in death. The symbolic bonding has the effect of releasing these women from the unfinished business or suppressed feelings going on in their lives.

As Brenda acted out her abortion from the baby's perspective, she was saying, in effect, "I know now what happened to you. I don't have to avoid it anymore. I don't have to not look at it anymore. I lived it as you lived it, and I know."

The release at that point is almost spiritual. It allows the woman to say "I, too, have suffered and I don't need to suffer any more."

Every woman I've counseled who has gone back through the abortion experience has found the pain diminished afterward. Brenda, for instance, never had visions of torn and broken babies again. She still had work to do. But in that psychodrama session she had broken her denial and healing had begun.

"Have You Had an Abortion?" Became a Standard Question

After counseling with Betty, Sue Ellen, and Brenda, I decided to inquire about abortion with all female patients who were suffering from the symptoms of lifestyle denial.

At first, I would ask, "How many pregnancies have you had?" but I found this was an ineffective question, because PAS women often didn't "count" their aborted pregnancies. One woman told me, for instance, that she had three pregnancies—two live births and one miscarriage. It wasn't until some time later that she shared she had also had three abortions.

When the indirect approach didn't work, I began asking the direct question "Have you had an abortion?" but burying it among other pregnancy-type questions and asking it matter-of-factly. Gradually, I developed a system of oral and written questionnaires that have proved invaluable to me as tools for diagnosing and treating PAS. These questionnaires are reproduced in Appendix E and their use will be detailed in chapter 6 of this book.

As I have shared these techniques with my colleagues, I have found that clinicians are often as reluctant to ask questions about abortion as patients are to answer them. Some fellow counselors have told me, "I can't ask that question." Or, "I can't ask that without making a value judgement on it—and we're not supposed to do that." Or "I won't ask the question; it isn't any of my business." Or, "It's irrelevant whether or not a woman has had an abortion—it's a dumb question."

My answer, based on my experience with Betty, Sue Ellen, Brenda and many, many others is: No question is dumb if it reveals the inner source of suffering! And PAS is too important an issue to be ignored.

If a woman can freely and openly discuss her abortion, if her memories of it are clear and she seems to have resolved her feelings about it, then of course we need to look elsewhere for the source of the symptoms. But we should never make that determination until we've asked the right questions and waited for and evaluated the responses.

Counselors can't give good counsel without obtaining good data. And we can't decide ahead of time what is and is not important. It's not a question of what's important to the counselor, but of what's important to the *client*. If coun-

selors are afraid of the questions or afraid they can't handle the answers, then they need to change career fields.
Otherwise, we're limiting ourselves to a practice of just
offering symptomatic pain relief when we could promote
real healing. It is important that we keep the ancient
Hippocratic Oath and "do thy patient no harm," but we
also need to avoid "doing thy patient no good." If we
aren't willing to delve beneath the surface and find the
cause of the malady, our treatments will be of little value.

3

The Mechanics of Denial

As I pointed out in chapter 1, denial is a normal defense mechanism that sometimes goes awry. It is an emergency bandage that gives a person time to get off the battle-field—putting off pain or trauma until a crisis is over and there is time to grieve.

But denial becomes a problem when it persists and prevents the normal grieving process from taking place. Instead of allowing normal grief to run its course, denial covers the pain and loss like a scab over an infected wound. Like an abscess that can't drain, the wound festers and the poison spreads throughout the system.

To use another metaphor, denial works like a tight cap on a well—it keeps everything under the surface. But repressed emotion, like water driven underground, eventually breaks out somewhere—usually in the form of self-destructive behaviors that, on the surface, may have little to do with the initial problem.

This kind of ongoing and destructive denial occurs whenever the day of reckoning after a traumatic experience doesn't come. This is most likely when the person who has experienced the trauma has no supportive environment in which to gradually process the pain he or she has experienced—as in the case of Vietnam vets with post-traumatic stress disorder. Unlike returning World War II veterans, who were complimented and praised for what they had done ("It's good you killed those Japs; they attacked Pearl Harbor! You're a hero!"), Vietnam vets were treated as visible reminders of a deeply unpopular war. At best, they were ignored; at worst, they were openly taunted and accused of atrocities. The "less stressful time" for coming out of denial never came, so denial became a way of life for them. Unfortunately, that ongoing denial also brought recurring nightmares, unexplained violent outbursts, substance abuse problems, and many other forms of dysfunctional behavior.

This kind of denial—and similar lifestyle dysfunctions—can also be found in aborted women with PAS. For such women, denial usually begins early in the abortion experience and continues long after it.

The denial that contributes to postabortion syndrome may include:

Preabortion denial
> of the pregnancy itself
> of responsibility for the pregnancy
> of the baby/POC's being human
> of what got her pregnant

Abortion denial
> of the physical experience itself
> of her emotional reaction to the procedure

Postabortion denial
> of certain aspects of the abortion
> of all memory of the abortion
> of relationship between the abortion and self-
>   defeating behaviors

This denial may be projected toward family, friends, counselors, and/or herself.

Preabortion Denial

Preabortion denial usually begins with "I can't be pregnant!" However, a condition like pregnancy is difficult to deny, and most women soon realize what the result will be without intervention. This is where a friend, family member, or a counselor at an abortion clinic may function as an "enabler" to help her *depersonalize* the event and deny her honest interpretation of what's happening in her body.

As mentioned earlier, language plays an important role in establishing and maintaining denial. Often the initial discussions are carried on in terms that are foreign to the pregnant woman. She may be told that she is not carrying a "baby," for instance, but a "mass of cells" or a "product of conception." The depersonalization may even extend to the woman herself. While she may have thought of the place where the pregnancy took place as a "womb," she may now find it referred to by the medical name, "uterus" or simply as "a conception vessel."

The people who do the initial interview at abortion clinics are *trained* to help depersonalize the experience. They are usually good at it, both because they believe what they are doing is right and because it's their job. But abortion clinic personnel are not the only ones who play this language game. Doctors, friends, family—even the woman herself—can do it. Unfortunately, such depersonalization can assist a reluctant woman to build denial rather than to face her situation honestly and make a decision that is consistent with her real feelings and convictions.

Having enabled the pregnant woman to disassociate herself from the baby/POC in her womb, the counselor or friend may move the attention from the POC/baby to the woman herself, stressing, in so many words, "It's your body, and it's your decision. You have several *alternatives* available." (It's good sales technique to shift the focus from "should I, or shouldn't I" to a look at the alternatives.)

The discussion proceeds, using clinical, legal, and technical language to describe emotions and body parts and situations that the woman may heretofore have spoken of using more traditional language:

Traditional Terms	Industry Terms
baby	product of conception
expecting	midterm
with child	fetal tissue
womb	conception vessel
abortion	postconception planning

The language transfer helps bring on denial because the woman *wants* it to work. This is a crisis pregnancy, and she *wants* an alternative to carrying it to term and raising a child. The terms, the matter-of-fact presentation of data, the quiet assurance on the part of the counselor that this is obviously what she wants to do—all reassure her. The woman can almost believe she is watching the event instead of participating in it.

If the transfer lasts, of course—and it sometimes does—PAS will be avoided. But problems come when the aborted woman recalls the event later without the benefits of the language transfer and the positive reinforcement.

What happens is that instead of changing her feelings, the pregnant woman has simply covered them with a layer of impersonal language. Just as a dichotomy of language has taken place, so has a dichotomy of feelings. Feelings are based on personal values and ideas and experiences, but they also grow out of our culture. In Western culture, our literature, folklore, and songs attribute nothing but pure, noble, self-sacrificing, and almost holy motives to mothers and, by inference, mothers-to-be. Mothers are expected to (and often do) give their lives to save their children. Being "in a family way" has traditionally been considered an enviable state. From the day they first knew a baby was growing inside them, women traditionally planned and prepared for its arrival with joyful anticipation. True, abortions were done in ancient times and were being done in our own time before the procedure was legal. Yet the mainstream of our society has traditionally considered a desire to end a pregnancy as outside the norm. That was our culture.

Now the pregnant woman is hearing from a variety of sources that it's okay *not* to have those feelings. She may even hear, "You probably shouldn't have them. After all, you're important, too. So are your husband/lover/parents/other children. *You* shouldn't have to carry this baby if you don't want it or if it would pose a hardship." Traditional morality said a woman sacrifices herself for her baby. Modern morality says there may be times when it is okay to sacrifice a baby/POC for the woman. Obviously, this is a highly charged, emotional issue. And I'm not making a value judgment on which argument is better—just reporting that they *are different.*

But the problem with these changing points of view is that sometimes the heart cannot process change as rapidly as the brain. Sometimes we make up our minds to follow a course of action that seems in our best interest, but we don't take into account the emotions that go with the action. This is what often happens with PAS-prone women.

The obvious question is, "If the woman is feeling reluctance, why does she go through an abortion?" There are two reasons. The first is fear of loss. She fears losing her husband—or, more often, her lover—her family, money, career, image, and freedom not only during the pregnancy, but also for the rest of her life. The second reason she goes through with it is that she is assured by respected sources (the medical profession, the provider of the services, many women's groups, and the media) that there are no after effects to the abortion. The result is that some women enter and leave preabortion with two conflicting sets of values, emotions, and language skills in place and denial is at work. Remember the young woman who held her abdomen when she ran so she wouldn't hurt the baby, even though she had already decided to abort the product of conception? Our PAS-prone woman is doing the same thing; she's holding onto two diametrically opposed philosophies!

The human mind is an amazing organ, and it *can* hold two opposing ideas at the same time—but the strain can become unbearable. This becomes clearer when we look at what happens when preabortion denial becomes abortion denial and postabortion denial.

Abortion Denial

Denial, once begun, is affected by exposure to added stressors that make it hard to continue the denial. Such stressors may include:

exposure to infants or other pregnant women
exposure to "right to life" material
discussions with family or friends
the actual reality of the abortion clinic or some other reminder of the reality of the abortion

If denial is broken *before* the abortion, of course, then the pregnant woman may simply change her mind about the abortion and there will be no PAS. However, once the abortion has taken place—or even during the abortion itself—the situation will be different. Then exposure to such stressors may actually *reinforce* the denial—because the woman finds breaking denial too painful.

This is especially likely if the abortion itself is painful. Abortion is often described as a safe and *painless* medical procedure. And for some women at a very early stage, the physical pain may indeed be minimal. However, most women who develop PAS say they experienced *considerable* discomfort and often severe physical pain. Moreover, because the *depersonalization* surrounding the abortion often extends to the patient, many of them report receiving little support or sympathy regarding that pain. They may have been told to "act like an adult" or that "it doesn't hurt; it's just a bit uncomfortable." They also report feeling that the medical personnel at the clinic seemed more concerned with speed than with comfort or caring. In the typical scenario leading to PAS, the woman was told to get up on the table and put her feet in the stirrups. She was strapped down and instruments were rather summarily inserted into the vagina and uterus. The feeling of "violation," or "vulnerability," coupled with unsettling sights and sounds, discomfort or pain, and perhaps sight of the aborted baby/POC, make for an unpleasant experience at best. (Some of my patients have referred to this as "mechanical rape" or "machine rape." At worst, the experience can be so traumatic as to powerfully reinforce denial.

In such cases, the trauma of the abortion translates what was becoming a very depersonalized experience into a highly personal and traumatic one. She doesn't want to think about it—ever—so she shuts it out. She drops it in the sea of forgetfulness and puts up a "No Fishing" sign, refusing to think about the abortion or what led up to it. Unconsciously, she is saying, "I can't handle these feelings, so I *don't* think about them. I don't express them. Instead, I push them down and away. I push away anything that reminds me of what happened."

Postabortion Denial

For the PAS woman, the process of denial continues after the abortion. Like the Vietnam vet, she is often given no societal support for processing what has happened to her, so she continues to deny the event, the feelings connected with the event, or both.

Keeping memories and feelings pushed under is hard work, but the alternative is too painful for the woman in denial to face. Thus she will avoid anything that threatens to bring back those repressed thoughts and feelings. One common aversion of the PAS woman is medical machinery, especially stirrups or anything that looks like or sounds like equipment she saw in the clinic. The sound of a vacuum cleaner or the suction straw at the dentist could bring back memories of the vacuum aspirator.

Some women in postabortion denial develop an aversion to sex, as it brings back memories of what happened in the abortion room. She lies on her back, she spreads her legs, and something is inserted into her vagina—just like *that* time. (These things don't always happen all at once or even consciously. A woman may feel revulsion at these things and not know why.)

The hot public debate over abortion can be a stressor that either breaks or reinforces postabortion denial. Abortion issues and pro-and-con demonstrations are routine fare in the media. Anti-choice/anti-abortion groups are fond of making their point with intrauterine photos of babies/POCs and statistics on fetal development. These groups have even been known to hand out life-sized plastic models of a baby/POC eleven to twelve weeks after conception.

One woman who eventually became a patient of mine was given such a plastic model as she left the abortion clinic. Later, she called her abortion clinic counselor and asked, "Are these accurate?" The counselor replied, "More or less."

The aborted woman said, "But it *looks* human!"

The abortion counselor laughed and replied, "They do look human—but they're not!"

The woman hung up the phone and dropped the plastic preborn baby/POC into the trash on her way for a bottle of Scotch. Within an hour, her denial was functioning again, but the stress of keeping the denial in place was breaking out in the form of alcohol abuse.

Lifestyle Denial

When memories and the feelings that go with them are pushed under or *suppressed*, the result is internal stress.

When they are suppressed long enough, they may actually become *repressed*. When this happens, the PAS woman may find that whole blocks of memory are missing; she may even block out the *entire event*. A woman in repression may not remember any of the details of her abortion nor be able to recall specific details even of the events and circumstances surrounding it. She may not even remember the exact year or season of the year! She may even react with hostility toward the therapist who probes into these issues!

At the end of this process, we have a woman who is severely emotionally depressed, who is building internal stress all the time with no way of alleviating any of it through normal expressions of grief. As a result, she becomes increasingly dysfunctional.

Initially, she may have looked away when she saw a baby/POC on television as developed as hers was at the time of abortion. Now she just mentally tunes out and isn't even aware that it's on. She has programmed herself to turn off anything that reminds her of the event. Denial has become an automatic process, like breathing.

She may find she has neither emotional highs nor emotions lows. She may once have worried about the "dead feeling" inside, but not now. Now she *expects* to feel that way. She has sex with no excitement and feels no concern when she doesn't have sex—or, as mentioned above, she may actively avoid sex.

At this point the aborted woman may show all the symptoms of lifestyle denial—substance abuse, compulsive behaviors, difficulty maintaining relationships, and so on. If she isn't treated, she can slide down the spiral of dysfunction at an ever-increasing speed, and she may not have a clue as to what is happening or why. Her emotions and perceptions are almost totally shut off.

A Conspiracy of Silence

If the PAS woman comes in three years later with depression, strained relationships, and lack of motivation, the clinician has no reason to suppose abortion is the primary cause of the problem. If we don't ask the right questions, we can waste a lot of time and allow a lot of lives to be wasted as well. Unless we're a *confident counselor*, we may not ask the right questions even if we do suspect abortion as a cause—because we know we're opening ourselves and the patient up for a highly charged emotional experience.

Patients don't volunteer the information because they're in denial. Counselors don't ask for the information because they're in a form of denial, too. Counselors deny there *should be* a problem or even *could be* a problem. They deny the need to probe a potential pain center. So a conspiracy of silence falls across the cause of the problems the woman is having . . . and we treat symptoms. We become enablers and allow patients to lead us off after will-o'-the-wisps, looking for other reasons for the pain they feel.

And so we say, "Perhaps you're depressed because you've broken up with your fifteenth boyfriend in the last two years." The patient agrees, "Sure, that's it. I can't seem to build a permanent relationship, and I really liked this guy." So we settle for that and deal with symptoms instead of trying to find out the *real reason why* she can't build a lasting relationship.

The deeper the denial, the greater a therapist's tendency may be to avoid what promises to be a painful experience for both client and clinician. However, if we back away from an issue because of fear or because we have made a mental-health diagnosis based on personal political persuasion, then I would say it's time to take down the diploma and change professions!

Detecting Denial

Detecting denial in a counseling situation is a delicate process. We have to probe as gently as a dentist, trying not to cause pain, but attempting to locate tender spots that indicate a problem.

One of the primary symptoms of denial is the inability to remember details about an event, so a counselor's first task will be to ask a series of gentle questions that may prod her memory. If a patient says, "I really don't remember anything about my abortion, I ask what she remembers about the *day*. What kind of a day was it? What did the office look like? What was the doctor wearing?

If that doesn't work, I ask, "Was it an *unpleasant* experience for you?"

If she says no, I ask, "Would you say it was a *pleasant* experience?"

Sometimes again she'll answer negatively. Well, it obviously was some kind of experience; it wasn't a nonevent. When a woman can't or won't remember, some kind of denial is at work. I will discuss the process of detecting and breaking denial in a later chapter. First however, I want to explore the normal process of grieving that in PAS is distorted by denial.

4

The Stages of Grief

Grieving is the natural—and healthy—response to loss. This process occurs naturally in most situations (such as the death of a family member) and is supported by society. It usually begins *immediately following the loss* and proceeds in a certain order—as shown in the classic "stages" described by Elisabeth Kubler-Ross:

Denial/Isolation "No, not me!"
Anger "Why me?!"
Bargaining "I promise not to do it again."
Depression "I've lost" "What's the use?"
Acceptance "I know this is going to happen."

It's different for a woman with PAS. She, too, has suffered a loss—of the baby/POC, of her time, perhaps of relationships. However, because of her denial, she is unable to proceed through the normal grief process.

Here, again, her predicament may be compared to that of a Vietnam veteran suffering from post-Vietnam stress disorder. The combat vet isn't sick because of the horror of seeing his buddy blown apart right next to him. He is sick because the horror of the event didn't allow him to process the loss of his buddy. The event itself was so stressful that he cannot bear his intense feeling of loss, his anger at the enemy, and his anger at the permanence of his loss. He therefore goes into denial and eventually shows symptoms of PVSD. The trauma didn't produce the illness. Rather, the trauma kept the logical steps of the grieving process from taking place, and *that* created the problem. The same is true for a woman suffering from postabortion syndrome.

The loss may have occurred some time before the problems related to that loss developed. Due to this time lapse and the fact that society is unwilling or unable to accept the need to grieve such a loss, an artificial grieving process often must be implemented in order for recovery to occur. I will explain techniques for "jump-starting" the grief process in a later chapter. But at this point I want to follow Kubler-Ross's natural grieving process and show how it applies to an aborted woman.

The Sequence of Grief

When my father died, I went through all the classic Kubler-Ross stages. I can remember his death as if it were yesterday, yet it was over twenty years ago. I had just got out of a three-year stint in the service and hadn't reestablished a close relationship with Dad. I was working in a clothing store a thousand miles from home when I got a call that he had suffered a heart attack. My brother said to me, "Terry, it's not serious, and there's no need for you to drive all the way here in the middle of winter."

I *wanted to go*, but at the same time, I had this great new career selling clothes. (That's how Harry Truman got started, and he went on to become president of the United States!) Then the next day, about ten o'clock in the morning, my brother called me at work. The phone was mounted to a column right in the middle of the store and I went to it when they announced on the loudspeaker that I had a phone call. Dozens of people were milling around me, and my brother came on the line. I said, "Hi, Jim." And he said, "Hi, Terry." Then he was quiet a moment. So I asked, "How's Dad getting along?" There was a pause and then he said, "Terry, Dad's gone."

My initial reaction was, of course, *denial!* There must be some mistake! Not *my dad*—not *me!* This is Terry, and the laws of the universe don't apply to me! I could tell that people were watching, so I just said, "I'll be home."

Jim said, "I don't think you should come home."

He was trying to save me a thousand-mile drive during a blizzard, but I had already moved from *denial* to *anger,* and I wanted to jump through the phone and throttle him! I yelled, "I *said* I will be home!" Now people were staring, so I hung up the phone, walked up the stairs and told my boss, "My dad died this morning. I'm going to have to go home for a few days." As I said those words, two tears rolled down my cheeks, one from each eye. Just that and nothing else. I was barely twenty-two, and I was proud of how I held myself together.

I went to my apartment, packed a few things, and gassed up the car. I drove like a New York cab driver and made the thousand-mile trip in two days. When I got home, my mother was beside herself, and the doctor was feeding her tranquilizers. My brother was calm and in control— but then, he'd had a chance to say goodbye. I was holding it in, but I was seething with anger.

On top of everything else, this was Christmas. Everyone else was planning big family gatherings around the Christmas tree. The Selbys would be gathering around Dad's casket. And it just seemed extremely unfair. The whole scene had an unreal quality about it, like a long, bad, boring movie. Denial was working for me; it was almost like it never happened. Yet I went ahead and helped make the funeral arrangements.

So far, what I was going through wasn't a lot different from what an aborted woman goes through. Initially, she's starts with *denial,* and she rolls with the flow as the professionals guide her into the right room and into signing the right papers. There's an unreal quality about it all, and she's keeping all her thoughts and feelings inside. *Maybe I should have this baby—but maybe I couldn't. Maybe I should; maybe I shouldn't. What's going to happen to me if I do? What will happen to me if I don't? Will I pay for this the rest of my life either way?* She's thinking all these things but not feeling them. She's managing her emotions through denial. Once again, a certain amount of denial is good in a crisis. It allows us to postpone grieving until another time when we can handle it. And then it breaks the grieving process into small, manageable bites. In fact, as I grieved my father's death, my denial continued to a certain extent. However, it did not prevent my moving ahead with the rest of the grieving process or feeling the necessary emotions—as it does with the PAS woman.

But though I was bouncing back and forth between denial and anger, I was moving more and more into the anger stage. I was mad at my father for dying. (The fact that anger is illogical doesn't necessarily diminish it.) I was mad at the doctors. (Maybe it was their fault my dad died!) I was mad at the hospital. I wanted to go and have it out with all of them.

Because I have a rather forceful personality, I *did* have it out with the doctors at the hospital the very next day—and with the people at the funeral parlor as well. I was like a wounded animal striking out at anything in the path.

The true source of the anger I was feeling was the recognition that I was helpless and that Dad's death was a permanent condition that I could not change. I would never again be able to say to my dad, "I love you." He would never again be there to offer me counsel and advice. He would never see my kids or hold them in his lap. We'd never go fishing again.

Dad's life was over. Our relationship had ended. Nothing I could do now would undo any of it. Just as nothing the woman who has had an abortion can do will bring back the baby/POC. It will not come back up the little vacuum tube and re-attach itself into her conception vessel and grow into a son or daughter. Now she has an extra burden, because she not only feels the *loss;* she also feels the *responsibility.* She chose for it to happen. Others may have encouraged her, they may have enabled her, but they didn't force her to come into the clinic and submit to the procedure. She made that choice.

Chances are, she's bleeding and hurting physically. She's also hurting psychologically. The greater the trauma of the event, the greater the psychological scars. Maybe she saw the baby/POC either as it was sucked down a tube or as the abortion center personnel wrapped it in saltwater-soaked towels and carried it away. Maybe she thinks it looked a lot more like a baby than it did a mass of cells. And she hurts. And she is angry. But if she's one of the unfortunate ones prone to PAS, she pushes those feelings down.

When my father died, *I* could tell somebody about my anger and hurt. My family stood with me. There were concerned professionals to guide me, to listen and nod wisely and say comforting things. Too often, the aborted woman has no one. Her experience is outside the realm of socially accepted grieving. She can't bring it up, and this is frustrating to her. This frustration may be directed at:

the people in the abortion clinic
the other person responsible for the pregnancy
pro-life/anti-choice people who bring it to mind

But often this frustration and anger builds and there's really no way to vent her feelings. After all, the abortion was her choice. She can't come back and say to her boyfriend, "You jerk! I'd like to pound your face in for making me do this just because you didn't want to be responsible for a baby!" And she can't pound her own face either. There are few support groups for her, and those that do exist aren't well known. So what does she do with her anger? She holds it in, and it begins to build—and built-up

anger can create or exacerbate just about every problem
known.

When we responsibly vent our anger and move on with
our grieving, the anger eventually subsides. Pent up anger
and continued denial don't offer that option. If I were still
writing angry letters to the funeral home about my dad's
death, everyone would agree that Terry Selby had a problem. If I played a game in my mind that it was all a mistake and my dad wasn't really dead, you'd say I needed
help. Yet the woman suffering from PAS feels just that kind
of unexpressed anger and is in just that strong a denial.
The longer and stronger she fights to keep it in, the greater
the eruption will be when it finally breaks out.

On the way back from my dad's funeral, I was still mad
and still in denial to a certain extent. I hurt, but I would
push the thought of that hurt down because I didn't want
to deal with it. Oh, I'd shed a tear now and then, but I'd
cut it off. I forced myself to think of something else. I'd
turn on the TV or radio to drown my thoughts.

At this point, I wanted to bargain. "Just let me wake up
and find this is all a horrible dream and I'll do anything for
you, Lord! I'll be a good son and I'll go to church and . . ."
But I sensed it was too late to bargain. Finally, *three months
later,* I sat down and cried like a baby. All the hurt and all
the guilt ("I wish I had . . ." and "I wish I hadn't . . .") came
gushing out. And I moved into the next stage, which is
sadness or depression. This stage involves the recognition
that the loss is permanent and it is forever. My dad was not
coming back, and it didn't do me any good to say, "Yes,
he's gone" intellectually unless I faced the fact emotionally
as well. And facing the fact meant feeling overwhelmingly
"down."

Finally, I began to come to terms with my dad's death.
Because I am a person of faith, I consoled myself that
although I truly missed him, I would see him again. In my
mind, I moved him from the grave where I left him to
heaven, where I believe he will be waiting for me. I arrived
at the final stage: *acceptance*—the ability to come to terms
with a loss and go on with life.

The woman suffering from PAS can't move to this stage of acceptance because she has never permitted herself to pass through the other stages. She has had nowhere to vent her anger, so instead of moving forward into the next stage, she has moved backward and returns to denial. Emotionally, however, she's in the other stages. She's angry and wants to bargain and feels depression, just as a person does in traditional grieving. But since she is in denial, the anger, the bargaining, and depression aren't aimed at the abortion incident and therefore can't be worked through naturally. They're aimed at anything and everything that comes by.

An Extra Step for the PAS Woman

To fully recover from her grieving process, it has been my experience that an aborted woman not only needs the five steps that Kubler-Ross described for grieving any loss, but also an additional step inserted between depression and acceptance. That step is dealing with *guilt and shame* and facing the problem of *responsibility*. Whether or not society, the counselor, or I believe she should feel responsibility, the PAS woman does. If she didn't already feel responsible, she wouldn't be suffering with postabortion syndrome.

Responsibility can take two roads: accidental responsibility and deliberate responsibility. If a woman accidentally backs a car over her baby, she experiences terrible guilt and remorse and grief because *she's responsible*. On the other hand, if she *intentionally* places her baby behind the wheel of the car and backs over it, she has a much more severe problem because she's *deliberately responsible*. This isn't to say that the loss of a baby/POC is as great as the loss of a child. It is to say that the woman feels *deliberately responsible* for what happened. That's a pretty gruesome conclusion—and it's why the denial is so strong. Her mind doesn't want to accept that feeling of responsibility. It's often more than she can process without outside help.

Table 1
Stages of Grief

KUBLER-ROSS	POSTABORTION SYNDROME	BEHAVIOR
Denial/Isolation	*Denial/Isolation*	*Denial/Isolation*
"No, not me."	"I did nothing wrong" or "I didn't have an abortion." "I feel nothing."	Doesn't talk about feelings or abortion procedure. Lies when asked if had abortion. Abuses drugs or alcohol to mask emotional pain. Overdoes other activities. Avoids film, TV and personal discussions about birth, life, abortion. Does not take a position on issues of life and death. Can't grieve other forms of separation, i.e., death issues. Denies owning any grief or feelings related to the death of baby/POC through abortion. Denies connection of other problems in her life and their relationship to abortion.
Anger	*Anger*	*Anger*
"Why me?"	"Why did this have to happen to me?"	Feels anger at self, the medical/legal system, the biological father, men in general, God, and so on. Lashes out at spouse, children, family. Experiences physical symptoms of pain in abdominal area, headaches, tension. Acts intolerant, irritable, rigid. Experiences relationship problems. Feels need to control situations. Develops compulsive behaviors, i.e., overeating, drug and alcohol abuse.
Bargaining	*Bargaining*	*Bargaining*
"I promise not to do it again."	"I'll never do it again if you make the pain go away. I'll work hard, then I won't feel anything. I'll really do special things for other kids and my own kids."	Change in philosophy of life and value structure. May adopt attitudes consistent with abortion as a means to put off grieving and emotional pain. Adopts a generally ambivalent attitude toward life; does not take a position on issues.
Depression	*Depression*	*Depression*
"I've lost."	"I can never change what happened. I'm	Has low self-esteem. Loses or gains weight. Withdraws from

desperate for somebody to tell me I'm okay. I am not lovable. I can never love the child I killed. I wonder if the child was/is in pain? I hurt as I remember the procedure. I am afraid the baby hurt when it was being torn apart or burned to death. Maybe I will be punished for the rest of my life for what I did."

friends and society. May think about or attempt suicide. Cries unexpectedly. Doesn't want to get up in morning. May change jobs or move suddenly. May continue to abuse drugs and/or alcohol. May have episodes of compulsive or manic behavior, i.e., cleaning, bathing, spending. Blames others for feelings; may divorce and/or change primary relationships. Has obsessive thoughts of the dead baby/POC. Loses sexual drive and romantic feelings.

Guilt/Shame

"I made the decision to kill my child. I am selfish and self-centered, and I hate myself. I cannot forgive my past. I should be punished for what I've done.

Guilt/Shame

Puts self down. Continues with self-victimizing behaviors. (Much like anger stage but a different issue. The issues of guilt/shame and personal responsibility are separate from the grieving process, but are best confronted during this period. At this point a turn must take place in the treatment process of the aborted woman. The experience of shame and guilt becomes the paramount therapy issue, and these are the feelings that need to be focused on so the mourning process can continue into the area of acceptance.)

Acceptance

"I know what is going to happen."

Acceptance

"I accept what I have done. Life was taken. The baby died at my hand. I have asked for forgiveness. Now I can go forward with my life. I am again able to feel sadness, joy, pain, mourning, etc. I can share my experience with others."

Acceptance

Speaks with other aborted women. Returns to meaningful relationships. Returns to religious activities if active prior to abortion. Gradually some spiritual awakening. Self-destruction is replaced with self-esteeming actions.

As harsh as it sounds, part of working through the grieving process of PAS is facing the perceived guilt. There's a certain amount of guilt involved in any death.

When my father died, I couldn't help wondering if he might have lived had I been a better son. That's normal guilt, and most people go through it in a normal manner. But the guilt would be much more severe if I'd killed my father, even accidentally. If I was responsible for my father's death, even if only in my mind, then there's a cause-and-effect relationship. I did something—he died.

It is that kind of cause-and-effect sense of responsibility that the aborted woman with PAS must work through. The guilt and shame she is feeling has to come out if healing is to progress. The general flow is depicted in table 1.

Without going through the stages, particularly the stage of guilt/shame, there can be no acceptance. There is merely the ongoing process of re-feeling and re-employing denial.

Once you've been through the steps of recognizing personal guilt and shame and responsibility, then you can begin to rebuild. Then not only the clinician but the patient knows the cause of the disease. Then and only then can real healing begin.

5

Victimization

Sir William Osler, known as the "dean of North American medicine," once said, "I have come to the place where I believe that most of our patients who recover do so because they have faith in the doctor's faith in the cure." What happens, then, when the cure the doctor prescribes harms the patient? What if the prescription causes pain instead of alleviating it? What if, in spite of a doctor's admonition from Hippocrates to "do thy patient no harm," the abortion creates more physical and emotional problems than the pregnancy?

When this happens, the postaborted woman is apt to feel anger and resentment. She may feel that the information she was given at the abortion clinic was not only erroneous, but also based on avarice or malice. She feels victimized, and these feelings intensify in direct proportion to the physical and emotional pain she has suffered.

Why would a mature woman (or sexually mature child) feel victimized by the abortion industry when she was also a participant in the decision? It has been written, "To whom much is given, much is required." Americans tend to hold the medical profession in high esteem and even awe. We are culturally geared to accept medical advice almost without question. If our car is malfunctioning and a mechanic says, "You need an overhaul and it'll run you about twelve hundred dollars," we get second and third opinions. If a physician says, "You have gallstones, and we're going to put you in the hospital and take them out next Thursday," we begin packing our bags. The patient has a high level of trust in medical practitioners, and when that trust is broken, a feeling of betrayal is not uncommon.

If a woman with a "problem pregnancy" comes into a family-planning or abortion clinic for counseling regarding a problem pregnancy and she's told, "Abortion is a safe, painless procedure that will solve your problem," she is predisposed to follow that advice. If, as a result of following that advice, she finds she suffers physical pain and emotional stress to such an extent that postabortion syndrome develops, then it's natural for the pendulum of trust and respect to swing in the opposite direction. When this happens, the medical team is perceived as being more interested in the fees for abortion than in the well-being of the patient.

People who feel victimized usually don't suffer in silence. Sometimes they want retribution or even revenge. In our society, a wide variety of courses, ranging from civil protest to civil disobedience and even civil legal action are available. However, since abortion is a private matter, the majority of women who have felt victimized have suffered in silence.

Will Abortions Someday Carry a Warning Label?

In the next few years, we could well see all abortion centers start issuing written warnings about pain and possible long-term effects to the procedure. Many are currently handing patients a few pamphlets, but I believe the trend will be toward formal, typed statements that must be signed by the patient prior to the abortion. These statements will require some deft legal handling because, under current law, while patients at any age are old enough to obtain an abortion, they must be eighteen years of age for a contract to be binding. There are three reasons for believing that warnings will become standard practice: It's good business; It could become the law; It could provide a legal shield against lawsuits.

If the PAS patients I've seen are any indication, it would seem that abortion centers must begin doing a better job of preparing their patients for the possibility of both physical and psychological pain. As more clinicians and patients become aware of PAS, informing patients of possible side effects will become more common. These are some reasons why.

1. *Better counseling is good business.* Some people doubt that *any* for-profit business would risk "losing a sale" to tell about the downside of a product or procedure. Yet pharmaceutical companies place "contraindications" in packets of prescription drugs and clearly defined warnings on over the counter (OTC) medications. Even a bottle of shampoo I opened the other night carried the words: "Warning: Do not get into the eyes. If you do, wash out." One would have thought, as the framers of the constitution so aptly put it, that such "truths" are "self-evident." Yet in our litigious society, someone decided that a warning that shampoo could irritate eyes would be prudent. We need only to compare the possible discomfort of an abortion against the possible discomfort of soap in our eyes to see that issuing a warning would be prudent policy.

    Because most companies are comprised of good people who want to do the right thing, and because doing the right thing truly is good business, I predict that the abortion industry will at least begin admitting the *possibility* of physical and emotional problems as a result of the procedure.

2. *It could become the law.* Those with an anti-abortion bias may doubt that an abortion center would ever willingly counsel about the down side of abortion. I feel they will, not only because I am convinced that it's the right thing to do. It's also the best thing to do from a public relationship. Should abortion centers fail to take voluntary action soon, I suspect that women with PAS and those who provide them with legal counsel could become a powerful force for political change. If women who have suffered from PAS should align forces with the anti-abortion/anti-choice groups *just as far as obtaining written warnings*, their action could bring about strict regulation of the industry.

   Historically, businesses and industries that have been unable to accept civic responsibility have been forced by law to comply. Most would rather comply voluntarily than have compliance forced on them. I believe this will be the case with the abortion industry.

   Of course, in some industries, there is always a feeling that it is best to "stonewall" reports of hurts and hazards. This was the early tack taken by those involved in the manufacture of asbestos products and Agent Orange and it is still the tack taken by the tobacco industry. Let us hope the abortion industry takes a different route.

3. *It could become legally indefensible to do otherwise.* Product liability laws generally hold that manufacturers are legally liable for damage incurred as a result of inadequate warnings or design flaws. Major damages have been awarded to those claiming to have suffered injury through the purchase of such impersonal products as automobiles, toasters, and toys. And nowhere is the tendency to sue and collect more evident than in the field of medicine. People are singularly unwilling to "forgive and forget" those who were held in high esteem and then broke trust with those who sup-

ported them. Fallen preachers, politicians, and physicians have proven fair game for the courts and the press.

Should just one woman out of every two hundred who have had abortions seek legal action due to alleged improper preparation or treatment, the courts would be logjammed. An estimated one million, seven hundred thousand abortions are performed each year in the United States.[1] Given the proper motivation and financial incentive, this could result in eighty-five hundred new malpractice cases filed each year. Even if the industry won every case, the cost in legal fees and lost time would be staggering, not to mention the adverse effect such suits had on malpractice insurance.

The Surgeon General's final draft report, "Medical and Psychological Effects of Abortion on Women," addresses the importance of unbiased and nonmanipulative counseling:

> The abortion decision is seldom made quickly or easily. Deciding to terminate a pregnancy often involves considerable personal ambivalence and emotional cost.
>
> Women who have had an abortion and later regret it have told me that they often recall their compulsion, at the time of counselling, to be rid of the problems resulting from the pregnancy; they also recall that they felt relief after the abortion.
>
> In retrospect, however, they say that they wish they had been better informed about the procedure, about alternatives to abortion, and about fetal development. It is possible that some of them were presented such information but their receptivity to that information may have been very much affected by the dilemma they faced.

I am convinced that eventually improved preabortion counseling will be available because of ethical, regulatory, and legal reasons, and fewer women will feel like victims.

However, that is *then* and this is *now*. The task of the clinical counselor is not to direct this feeling of victimization
into one channel or the other, but to help the woman come
to grips with it.

Who Is Likely to Feel Victimized?

Most often, those who feel victimized by abortion are
single young women.[2] A woman feels she has to face a
problem pregnancy alone and seeks a social solution for a
personal problem. She inquires about a medical solution, is
assured it will solve the problem, and follows "doctor's
orders." Later, she sometimes finds she merely replaced
one problem (the pregnancy) with another (postabortion
syndrome). She feels someone sold her a solution that
didn't work, that she was lied to, taken advantage of, and
misled.

Suppose you bought a car and was told it would run
one hundred thousand miles, but the engine failed after
only twenty thousand miles. Suppose you found there was
no warranty and the one who sold you the car denied all
responsibility for what happened. After all, it was *your
decision* to buy the car! You seek help and are told to think
happy thoughts and get involved in other activities (such
as hiking). Would you be hurt? Would you feel angry?
Would you feel victimized?

Imagine how the woman with PAS feels. The item she
bought (the abortion) did not do what it was supposed to
do (give her a better, happier life and solve her problems).
Moreover, she had physical pain and emotional pain as
well. To top it off, there's no way to "fix" the situation and
no recourse. Even without trying to tie in moral implica-
tions, it's not difficult to find why the woman with PAS
feels victimized.

In general, the feeling of victimization comes about
when women feel they have been misinformed:

about what is being aborted[3]
about the objectivity of the counseling at the clinic[4]

about the physical pain of the abortion

about the psychological pain of the abortion

about the emotional after effects of the abortion

So far we have focused on the *aborted woman,* yet a sense of victimization can affect others as well. This is much more rare, because physical and emotional pain can't really be comprehended secondhand. Also, abortion is usually a private matter that isn't discussed with family or friends. However, as the circle of involvement widens, the feeling of victimization can spread. It can affect an entire family, as we'll see in our next case history.

Case History: Margaret MacDonald

The typical woman with PAS is single and young at the onset of symptoms. Margaret MacDonald was neither. Happily married to her childhood sweetheart, she was in her mid-thirties and had three children. She and her husband had discussed having another child someday, but they weren't ready when Margaret became pregnant with what would have been their fourth child. They went to an abortion counseling center and then made a decision to have an abortion. Because they didn't want anyone in town to know, they went out of town. And because they could afford the extra expense, they went to a hospital-based clinic.

Margaret checked in early in the morning and had her abortion. After a brief stay for observation, she was given a variety of pamphlets and sent home. They got in the car and, as her husband drove, she read the pamphlets. Before they had gone thirty miles, she began hemorrhaging. Her husband rushed her back to the hospital. She was sent first to the emergency room, where it was found that the abortion had perforated her uterus and bowel. Poisons were now coursing through her system, and her life was in jeopardy. They rushed her into the operating room and performed emergency surgery, repairing the bowel and removing her uterus. For two weeks they battled infection as she hovered near death. In fact, on two separate occasions, she had to be resuscitated.

I saw Margaret and her husband four years later. They felt victimized by the referral agency, by the hospital, and by the doctor who performed the abortion and examined her afterward. She had been told abortion was a safe and simple procedure. The counselor had told them, "It's no big deal." To Margaret and her husband, it *was* a big deal. It was like going in to get a tooth pulled and having your head torn off. They were traumatized. She almost lost her life, and they would never be able to have another child.

A sense of frustration and feelings of victimization are common after any botched surgical procedure. However, the anguish the MacDonalds felt went much deeper than that. They deeply felt the loss of that baby/POC and both were suffering the classic symptoms of post-traumatic stress disorder as a result of their abortion experience. Of course, they didn't come in to discuss *this* problem, they came in because they were having marital problems and she was depressed.

Obviously, the MacDonalds are an unusual case. For one thing, they are a mature, stable couple. For another, they underwent a lot of physical and emotional trauma as a result of the procedure. And the facts show that the greater the physical pain, the greater the likelihood of PAS developing. Yet it would be surprising if they *didn't* feel victimized by the abortion process. Both had to go through extensive counseling before they were again fully functional.

Case History: The Darbys

The Darbys were a textbook-typical American family, the kind frequently found in fiction but so seldom in fact. Mr. Darby worked outside the home, and Mrs. Darby was a full-time homemaker. After twenty years of marriage, they were still sweethearts and best friends. They were hard working, honest and the pillars of their church and community. Politically conservative, they were liberal in their caring and sharing with others. They were the kind of people everyone would like to have for neighbors.

The Darbys had two teenage daughters and a pre-teenaged son. One of the daughters, whom we'll call Pat, was a junior. The other, Ann, was a sophomore. John, their son, was in the sixth grade. Both girls did well in school and were active in athletics. Beyond the usual problems of bills, boyfriends, and growing pains, they were a happy family.

Then, in the fall of her junior year, Pat became pregnant. The boyfriend suddenly lost all interest, and she was left to face her predicament alone. Because a pregnancy out of wedlock didn't fit into their lifestyles, she ignored the situation as long as she could. Finally, in her fifth month, she came and told her mother privately. Mrs. Darby, who had always deferred judgment on major matters to her husband, decided to handle this one herself. She was very pro-choice/pro-abortion and told her husband that their daughter needed an abortion.

Mr. Darby, who had a strong anti-abortion/anti-choice bias, balked. Mother persisted. She calmly explained that they wanted Pat to go to college and that a baby at this point would mean the end of that dream—not to mention hurting her chances of finding a good husband. Besides, for Pat to support the child, they would have to care for it while Pat worked and Mrs. Darby felt they were too old to raise another child. Finally, she argued, an illegitimate child in the family would ruin all of them socially. She repeated to her husband the lines she had read so often in pro-choice literature: "Abortion is safe, painless and simple—and no one will ever know."

Mr. Darby reluctantly agreed, and the three of them went to an abortion clinic for counseling. Because of the late term, the abortion had to be done by saline injection in a hospital-based clinic. After two saline injections and a difficult labor, the baby/POC was delivered, still showing signs of life. It was promptly removed, and no one in the family ever knew (or asked) what happened next, but a death certificate for a "female infant" had to be signed.

After the abortion, father and daughter were devastated. They felt they had murdered a baby, a baby that hadn't wanted to die, but had fought for her life before either the saline or the hands of the staff had ended it. Pat's mother was more clinically detached—maybe it was a baby, maybe it wasn't. The main thing was the problem was solved and no one would ever know about it.

But the former boyfriend knew, and he bragged about "getting his old girlfriend knocked up." A classmate came up to Ann and said, "Hey, I heard Pat had an abortion!" Ann was stunned. The family secret that had been kept from her was common knowledge at school.

The relationship between the two sisters deteriorated. Ann had always idolized Pat; now she resented her for killing the child that would have been Ann's niece. Before, Pat and Ann had been friends and done things together. Now they were strangers. Pat went to pot—literally as well as figuratively. She began to abuse drugs and eat compulsively. She changed her appearance, changed her friends, changed her goals. She became a "wild child," no longer interested in school or college, athletics, or church. Deep inside, Pat felt the abortion was a mistake, but she was in denial—so she buried herself in pro-choice work to reaffirm the rightness of her decision.

Pat needed help, but her mother denied there was a problem "It's just a stage," Mom said to family and friends. "She'll outgrow it. All kids seem to be going through some sort of rebellion nowadays."

The whole family began to change. Ann became a perfectionist—a superachiever in school, in church and in the community. The parents, who had always been active in community and church activities, now both dropped out entirely. They retreated into the fortress of their home and raised the drawbridge, not venturing out unless absolutely necessary. Their world, which had once been quite large, shrank to include just the two of them—and frequently they weren't speaking to each other.

Years went by. Mr. and Mrs. Darby's relationship became a marriage in name only; the only thing they had in common was their children. And since they didn't feel Ann needed any attention, they focused all their care and attention on Pat, who obviously did.

Pat's life continued its downhill slide. In addition to overeating and abusing drugs and alcohol, she became a compulsive gambler, and her parents covered her losses time after time, eventually almost destroying themselves financially to "bail her out." She lost a long series of jobs and was always on her parents' doorstep with financial problems. By this time, she was married and had two children, but her husband was also a substance abuser and the marriage had been in trouble from the beginning. Pat had made two suicide attempts and talked about suicide frequently.

Her parents lived in a state of frantic worry about Pat. They paid off her debts and bought her cars, clothes, and other material things to fill her life, but nothing seemed to help.

Finally, *fifteen years after Pat's abortion*, Mr. and Mrs. Darby sat down one evening and began talking. They admitted how unhappy they had become. Perhaps it would be better to split the property and try to find some measure of individual happiness in whatever time they had left. It was a discussion of options, dispassionately presented without emotion or love. With clinical detachment, they weighed the relative financial security they had as a couple against the possibility that they might find happiness apart. Having decided financial security was important to them, they agreed to seek counseling to see if their marriage could be put back together. That is when they came to see me.

As I worked with the Darbys to untangle the threads of their lives, we began to look back to a time when their marriage was working. They talked wistfully of the "Camelot years," when the girls had been active in school, when they had been active in church and community, when they had cared for each other. A clinical social worker who sees a healthy situation degenerate into an unhealthy one looks for a root cause. So I began to probe gently, asking questions with studied casualness while watching for signs that I had touched on a tender spot in their lives.

We had already talked about the couple's more recent problems—clearly a source of hurt and bitterness. But the problems had begun earlier. Having exhausted all other possibilities, I took a shot in the dark. "Has there been an abortion in the family?" I asked casually.

The reaction was electrifying. Mrs. Darby tightened her lips and glared at her husband with a "Don't you dare!" look. Mr. Darby put his head in his hands and cried like a baby.

I was startled. He was a big man, a man used to dealing with other big, tough men in the construction trade—and there he was crying like a child. Finally he reached for a tissue, blew his nose, and sobbed, "We killed our granddaughter!"

He composed himself and told the whole story. All the time he was talking, his wife was just sitting there looking at him. She was angry and embarrassed; the look on her face clearly said, "I can't believe he's doing this!" Seeing the expression on her face, he became angry himself.

The pain and the anger were so intense that I assumed the abortion must have happened recently. I asked, "When did this happen?" To my surprise, she answered, *"Fifteen years ago."*

I turned to Mrs. Darby and said, "He seems upset by this abortion. How do you feel?"

She never blinked. "I'm pro-choice and it was the only choice to make," she said firmly, then added, "It's a woman's right to decide what she ought to do with a pregnancy, and we don't need any unwanted children in the world. Besides, God and I have worked this out." I couldn't help wondering why Mrs. Darby found it necessary to "work it out with God" if there was no perceived problem. However, counselors do not enter into debates with clients, so I did not challenge her statement.

In their previous descriptions of their troubles, the Darbys had mentioned Pat's behavior problems, but this was the first indication they had given as to a possible cause. In fact, after their first few sessions, they had become convinced I should counsel Pat and were paying for her sessions.

Now that news of Pat's abortion had leaked out, Mom showed the first emotion I had seen other than anger. She nervously pleaded, "Now, when you see Pat, don't bring this abortion up to her. She just can't handle it, she's suicidal."

I said, "No, this is the very thing we *have* to bring up to her. If it's at the root of her problem, she won't get better until we've handled it."

Mrs. Darby snapped, "She doesn't want anyone to know!" Then she added, grudgingly, "But you do what you think is best. You probably will anyway." I couldn't help wondering if she expected me to do the opposite of what I thought was best, but again said nothing.

During Pat's next appointment, I did bring up the subject of the abortion. Pat's reaction was much like her father's; grief, agony, heartache, and despair poured out at the mention of that act fifteen years ago. Since her problems had begun right after the abortion, I felt at last I had a handle on the source of Pat's compulsive behavior, as well as her family's problems. Now the process of healing could begin. Gradually, over the course of our sessions, Pat began to get in touch with her feelings and to grieve the loss of her baby as she would grieve any death. As we worked through the grieving process, Pat began to improve.

As shown in the previous chapter, an important part of grieving in cases of PAS is handling the personal responsibility for the act that caused the problem. This is more difficult when the woman with PAS was an adolescent when the abortion occurred. As children (in the sense they are beneath the legal age of responsibility), they are very susceptible to the advice and counsel given them by their abortion counselor or, more rarely in abortion cases, their parents.

The responsibility for Pat's abortion lay on her but also on her parents, particularly her mother. Therefore, while accepting personal responsibility was important to Pat's healing, it was absolutely vital to bring healing to her parents.

When we discussed this concept with Pat's parents, Mrs. Darby continued her denial. She insisted that they had gone ahead with the abortion merely for Pat's sake. Otherwise, her reputation would have been ruined, she couldn't have gone to college, she wouldn't have been able to make a good marriage. Of course, all these things had happened anyway, but Mom just couldn't see it that way. Finally, however, both she and her husband were able to admit that the decision had been made for Pat because of the perceived benefits *to them*—not *to her*. They were the ones who had been worried about the loss of free time in keeping the child, about the embarrassment, and so on. And like characters in a Greek tragedy, they had drifted inexorably into all the terrible situations they were fighting to avoid.

When Mr. and Mrs. Darby began to talk about and accept responsibility for what they had done, they were able to grieve. And then their own marriage began to heal. Pat was getting well. Her parents were getting better. Yet there was one more victim who needed to be treated: Ann, the "good daughter." Now her parents arranged for her to come in for counseling as well.

Ann had felt a deep anger with her parents and her sister over the abortion. Why hadn't she been told? Why did she have to find out about the abortion at school? Why had she been denied the niece she wanted? Yet she had reacted to her anger and grief in a totally different way than either her sister or her parents. She had become perfect. She was "Miss Clean," never fooling around, never wasting time; always giving, never demanding anything.

As Mr. and Mrs. Darby had become more and more involved with "helping" Pat through a long series of problems, Ann's anger had increased. She had felt, not without some justification, that the *bad* daughter got everything and the *good* daughter got nothing. Ann loved her family, but she didn't like them very much. Ann had moved away from home as soon as possible because she couldn't stand living with her family.

But Ann's problems hadn't stopped when she moved on. Her perfectionist tendencies made it impossible to develop a romantic relationship: no man was good enough. (This was also partly due to resentment of her dad, who hadn't stood up for what he and she had believed was right.) In addition, she felt a constant inner conflict over the suffering her family was going through. On one hand, she felt they deserved what was happening to them because they had deliberately and selfishly chosen to do something she was convinced was wrong. On the other hand, she felt compassion for them because she really loved them. Torn between these feelings of condemnation and compassion, she buried herself in religious and pro-life/anti-choice work, hoping to "save someone else's baby" and spare another family the suffering hers was going through.

Ann felt, not without reason, that her family had two existences: a public one and a private one. Publicly, things were fine, but privately the unacknowledged death of her niece was tearing them apart. What she didn't realize was that she, too, had a public and a private existence. On the outside, she was happy and confident but inside she was unhappy and insecure and falling apart—not only because of her own unforgiveness, but because she missed that niece terribly. She grieved the loss even more than her sister did—perhaps even more than her father. Eventually,

each member of the family had to go back through and
grieve the death of the baby and resolve their anger at one
another. Ann had never discussed her feelings with Pat.
Now she had a chance to do that. She shared her feelings,
her resentment, her concern and her love for her
sister—*and forgave her.* Ann had never shared her hurt over
being neglected by her parents—together they had to deal
with that. Mr. Darby had to deal with his resentment
toward his wife over the abortion. She had to deal with her
resentment toward him over related matters.

This all happened three years ago. It would be pleasing
to report that all the wounds are healed and everyone is
healthy and happy. The truth is that the wounds *are
healing,* but they are not totally gone. The wounds ran deep
and were allowed to fester for a long, long time. While the
family is healing and everyone is health*ier* and happ*ier*
than they were, each has a way to go. The important thing,
however, is that they realize this. They are committed to
going the distance—together.

Where are they today? The parents have gone from a
cold war to being a loving and supportive couple. Ann has
forgiven her parents and her sister. Today, she is happily
married with children.

Pat has had ups and downs, but the trend line has been
up. For instance, she used to go absolutely crazy each year
on the anniversary date of the abortion. Well, in the last
couple of years, she hasn't gone *as crazy.* She calls up and
says, "I'm at the anniversary date again and I'm losing my
mind." We talk through it for a few days in a row and she
gets through it.

The point is, the Darbys have gotten over their feelings
of victimization. Each, in their own way, has accepted their
own responsibility for the problems in their lives and has
taken responsibility for working together to solve those
problems.

6

Breaking Denial

Breaking denial is a painful process for the counselor and the counseled. However, until the woman with PAS actually comes in contact with the pain she is trying to cover up, no healing can take place.

There are three steps in breaking denial. The first step is to aid the counselee in recalling and remembering the event that caused the problem—the abortion itself and the emotions connected with that event. The second step is to bring the counselee to a point where she can accept and resolve the loss. The third step is to bring her to a point of ownership, where she can accept responsibility for the effect the abortion had on her life and relationships.

Step One in Breaking Denial: Remembering

The Event

The first step in breaking denial, *remembering,* is the least value laden but the most painful part of the entire process. These memories can range from painful preabortion discussions that she had with family members, friends, and associates to actual recollections of the procedure and its aftermath. Because the aborted woman has found these memories and the attached emotions too disturbing to process, she has pushed them to the back burners of her mind or even repressed them entirely. Bringing these memories to the forefront cannot help but be painful, but it is crucial to the healing process. I have found that it is somewhat less stressful if we keep the interview casual, showing I care yet keeping a discreet, "clinical detachment." Since most women find a form questionnaire nonthreatening, I include an abortion history with the initial background packet and have the client fill it out before the first interview. (See Appendix E for a copy of the form.)

The questionnaire is a simple, nonthreatening data gathering device and most women have no problem filling it out. Of course, the stronger the denial, the less likely the patient is to be willing or even able to recall the details. Thus, a very sketchily filled out form is a clue to the counselor that denial may be present.

One woman in her early thirties came to me because of long-term depression resulting in, or exacerbated by, an inability to maintain intimate relationships. She left the abortion questionnaire entirely blank, explaining she had never had one. We began discussing some of her initial sexual contacts during adolescence in an attempt to discover what some of them meant to her and to learn whether any of them might be affecting her now. Then suddenly, right in the middle of our discussion, she stopped, turned her face to the window, and began to weep silently. I asked what she was experiencing or remembering. She wiped her eyes and said, "I had forgotten that I had an abortion when I was seventeen."

As this patient began discussing her abortion, it became clear to her that she had been suffering as a result of that experience. She was amazed that she had literally and totally forgotten not only the facts surrounding the abortion—*but the abortion itself!*

Denial strong enough to block out an entire incident is

relatively rare. More typical is the woman I counseled who vividly recalled the two-hundred mile trip she and her boyfriend made to the abortion clinic. She remembered getting out of the car and going up the steps—*but had absolutely no memory of what happened inside!*

We backed up and focused on the car trip. Little by little she revealed the details of that journey. She remembered hoping her boyfriend would stop her or show some reluctance. She remembered wanting to scream, to cry, to jump out of the car and run. And she remembered making a conscious decision to push these thoughts out of her mind—forcing herself to think of other things, to let her mind go blank, to detach herself from both the process and the procedure. Consequently, by the time she opened the clinic door, she was already in denial. She forced herself to think of other things throughout the abortion and then later forced herself to never think of it again.

If the PAS patient can't recall any portion of the abortion procedure (what happened before, during or after the actual procedure) I have found it helps to orally go through a set of questions with them. (See Appendix E for a copy of the questions.)

1. *Avoidance.* Simple avoidance is the most common behavior. Usually, the patient will simply change the subject from the abortion to another, less painful, topic. "What did the room look like? It had green walls. I remember my sister in Omaha used to say that green was a. . . ."

2. *Inappropriate emotions.* It is not unusual for a PAS woman to exhibit a totally inappropriate emotion when a counselor approaches a painful memory. I can remember a PAS woman who began to laugh uncontrollably as she described the other patients in the abortion waiting room, the preabortion counseling, and even the procedure itself. Inappropriate emotions such as laughter, subdued hostility, repressed anger,

subtle withdrawal, and so on are all forms of denial, of covering up, of refusing to face painful facts.

3. *Inappropriate behavior.* Inappropriate behavior is another common smoke screen to cover denial. It's not uncommon for a PAS woman's legs to begin shaking while describing her abortion. The shaking is the mind's way of drawing attention to some other activity to prevent us from continuing the discussion of the abortion experience.

4. *Overt hostility.* Overt defiance and hostility are other common reactions. "I didn't come here to talk about that! If that's what you want to talk about, there are plenty of other counselors!" I've had clients become red in the face and yell, "My abortion *is not* my problem!" Since people seldom get that hostile about things that don't bother them, I call this hostility a "snarl reaction." It's the same kind of growl you get when you approach your pet poodle to remove a thorn from her paw. The growl isn't directed at you, it's directed at the thing causing pain. It's a way of saying, "Be careful! I'm hurting there!"

5. *Overt withdrawal.* At the other end of the emotional spectrum is withdrawal. Withdrawal may take many forms. Answers may be reduced to a monosyllable, or they may cease altogether. The underlying rationale is, "If I don't say anything, maybe this discussion will stop."

The Emotions

The casual questions, coming methodically one on top of the other, chip away at the defensive mechanism. It's a slow process, but denial is broken off bit by bit until the entire event has unfolded. This is usually too lengthy and too intense a process for a single counseling session. Yet it is important not to end the session without allowing the patient to see *some victory.* She will be encouraged to see that she has identified the cause of the problem and is making some progress toward recovery.

Overcoming the denial of *events* also involves overcoming denial of the *emotions* related to those events. The raw emotions usually surface when the woman begins sharing the thoughts that came to her during the abortion: These thoughts may be directed toward herself, the baby/POC, the clinic staff, or even God:

> "I've done the unspeakable. I can't ever talk about this to anyone."
>
> "Goodbye, little one! I hope you understand why I have to do what I'm doing. Please don't hate me!"
>
> "No, stop—I can't go through with this! You lied to me! It hurts! I *can't* be still; I want off this table! Stop!"
>
> "Please, God, forgive me. Please don't let the baby suffer too much."

The feelings involved in an abortion can be very intense, far too intense to be processed at the time of the abortion. In fact, it is *because* these feelings are so intense that denial sets in as a normal protection mechanism. But if the denial persists, the woman will be unable to process these feelings later. The denial of these feelings keeps her from going through the normal grief process and thus prevents her from healing.

Uncovering emotions that have been denied is not an easy task for the clinician. As the case histories mentioned earlier show, some women scream as they tell about their abortion. I've known them to break down and cry and writhe on the floor in agony. (We soundproof our counseling rooms.) Some have fainted as they reached the point of telling about the actual abortion. On a couple of occasions, the patient had a dissociative break and lost touch with reality while discussing the abortion event. (The psychotic breaks have been very similar to those sometimes experienced when a patient shares an incestuous act.) This hap-

pened to a patient I'll call Marian. I was "going through
the questionnaire," asking the questions on my list. But
when Marian tried to answer my question about getting
onto the abortion table, she fainted and had to be revived!
After a few moments, she continued. Her breathing
became shallow, and she whispered, "When I think about
it, it's like I'm losing touch with reality! It's like I'm having
a hard time staying on the earth. I feel like I'm falling
down a white tunnel." Then she fell silent, and I called out
to her more and more loudly. Finally, she responded, saying, "I can hear you, but it's like it's far away, and I have to
really concentrate on it."

Later, Marian revealed she had similar dissociative experiences whenever she thought about her abortion and often
when she had sexual intercourse (which triggered memories of what had happened in the abortion center.) Once we
broke through her denial, these episodes never returned.

Step Two in Breaking Denial: Acceptance of Loss

The second step in breaking denial is accepting the fact
that there has been a loss. This acceptance comes when the
woman has been through the procedure, has remembered
the details, and can discuss it with appropriate feelings.
This isn't to say that she finds the discussion *easy* or *pleasant*—simply that she is able to discuss and describe them
in detail. It is only when she can recall and remember that
she can deal with the fact that she lost something that was
important to her.

When I shared my feelings about the death of my father,
I told how I finally came to the point where I realized I had
lost something important to me. If I had remained unable
to think about my father or had tried to maintain denial
that he was important, then I could never have broken
denial. In the same manner, a woman who suffers from
PAS feels she has lost something important. (I've never
known a PAS patient who felt the loss was a POC, it's
always a baby—otherwise, she wouldn't be a PAS patient.)

She must acknowledge that loss in her own mind before she can move through the healing process. It is our task as counselors to help her deal with the loss issue.

Step Three in Breaking Denial: Ownership of Responsibility

The third step in breaking denial is ownership of responsibility. The woman must transfer responsibility for the abortion from the doctor, boyfriend, spouse, friends, pressures, circumstances, and so on, to herself. She must own her actions by admitting, "This is something I *chose to do*. Maybe other people encouraged me to do it, but it was *my decision*. If harm was done, *I did it*. If wrong was done, *I am responsible*." As long as she can delude herself into thinking, "It really wasn't my fault," she will be stuck in denial—and she will be unable to move through the grieving process. (In cases of adolescent abortion, like Pat's, ownership of responsibility is often shared. Even in those cases, however, the PAS patient must accept her own degree of responsibility for the abortion.)

In a sense, this issue of facing responsibility is the bottom line in the process of breaking denial. We all have a natural tendency to rationalize our mistakes and misdeeds by saying, "It's not (or wasn't) my fault. "Everything I do that's wrong is someone else's fault," Anna Russell wrote in "Psychiatric Folksong." Comedian Flip Wilson does several routines built around the lame excuse, "The devil *made me do it!*"

Healing for any serious problem can't come until we acknowledge personal responsibility for what has happened in our lives. We are the ones to blame. As Harry Truman used to say, "The buck stops here." The guilt rests squarely on our shoulders.

One of the primary causes of mental problems is guilt, and the reason we so often *feel guilty* is that *we are guilty*. If our patients feel guilty, therefore, we must help them deal with that guilt using standard counseling practices and procedures or we haven't helped them with their problem.

At this point, the clinician's goal is to help the patient realize *she* has some personal responsibility in what happened and to assist her in facing the guilt feelings that go with that responsibility. Fully coming to terms with this responsibility will come later, during the grieving process. But it is important that she understand from the beginning that the responsibility is at least partially hers and that the clinician will be wanting to deal with it later.

The Clinician's Role in Breaking Denial

In summary, the clinician's role in breaking denial is to:

assist the patient in remembering

assist the patient in facing feelings of loss and victimization

assist the patient in facing personal responsibility and guilt feelings.

The reason for the lengthy examination is to locate the point of the patient's pain. To find out where the hurt is, a physician must ask diagnostic questions. So must a counselor, clinician, pastor, priest, psychologist, or psychiatrist.

The diagnostic questions suggested in this book are merely tools with which a clinician can push, probe, tap, and pull to see if the emotions and feelings surrounding the event are healthy and sound. To be effective, they must be used gently and nonjudgementally. This is true in all types of counseling, of course, but it is particularly important when dealing with the postaborted woman. She already wants to deny the event. Any hint of shock, dismay or condemnation on the counselor's part will push her even farther back into denial.

I recommend that the oral questions in Appendix E be used after the clinician has identified that the patient has had an abortion and feels there is a possibility the abortion experience is causing or contributing to the problem. While it is not the counselor's job to make a value judgment on whether or not the abortion was a good idea or should or should not have been done, we do need to keep in mind some impossibilities:

> You can't be an alcoholic if you've never taken a drink.
>
> You can't be an incest victim unless a family member has violated you.
>
> You can't have post-Vietnam stress disorder if you never left the United States during the Vietnam war.
>
> You can't have postabortion syndrome without an abortion experience.

Just as the counselor's personal attitude about liquor, Vietnam, incest, and abortion shouldn't interfere with his or her ability to diagnose and treat alcoholism, PVSD, and incest, the counselor's opinion on abortion should not color his or her response to PAS.

Why It Is Important to Break Denial

The woman with PAS needs to "revisit and relive" the abortion because her denial has kept her from finishing the abortion experience. This means she has denied herself the opportunity to grieve and hence to heal. As noted earlier in this book, aborted women are often not allowed the conventional methods of handling loss—a funeral to emphasize the reality of the loss, the opportunity to "talk out" her grief, the support of the community, and spiritual solace. As a result, it is easy for aborted women to "get stuck" in denial.

We can each manage a certain amount of "unresolved grief" or "unfinished business." In PAS cases, however, the amount of stress exceeds this threshold and plays havoc with a woman's life. This stress must be relieved before she can get on with living her life. And the first step in relieving this stress is breaking denial.

Denial, once broken, may surface again during the grieving process as her mind attempts to shield her from the hurt of a traumatic event. The clinician should look at this as a temporary aberration, not as a relapse into total denial. In my experience, I've found breaking denial is like breaking a horse—once it's broken, it may rear up from time to time, but it knows its limits. Once the woman with PAS has broken her denial, grieving—and healing—can begin.

In most instances, grieving begins immediately after denial is broken, because once the loss is faced, it is natural to grieve that loss. Occasionally, however, grieving doesn't spontaneously occur immediately after denial is broken. Since grieving is vital to the healing process, when this occurs, the clinician has to "jump start" the grieving process. This is discussed in greater detail in the next chapter.

7

Guiding the Grieving Process

There is nothing new about grief. Grieving began as Adam and Eve left the garden, reached gigantic proportions at the death of Abel and has continued throughout our history. As noted in earlier chapters, there is a definite process to grieving. We get ready to grieve. We grieve. Then we either move on or we don't. If we move on, the intensity of the pain gradually subsides. If we don't move on, then our pain remains intense. If we deny that grieving needs to be done, we short-circuit the whole process.

Grieving is important because it enables us to complete an unpleasant event in our lives. If a woman is still setting a place at the table for her husband who died ten years ago, most clinicians would agree that *she has a problem*. If a Vietnam veteran still plans fishing trips with a buddy that was killed in action, we would all agree *he has a problem*. But when an aborted woman seems to be having problems because of an abortion ten years earlier, most clinicians say *she shouldn't have a problem*.

At the risk of beating a dead horse to a double death, let's reiterate that whether or not a clinician feels a woman should be having a problem is irrelevant. What *is* relevant is that she *is having a problem.* She's having trouble dealing with a real life experience and she needs help. In that regard, treating a patient with PAS should be no more or less threatening than treating a patient who has lost a father or mother, a child, or a friend.

We would all agree that on hearing the word *abortion,* the clinician shouldn't stand and point an angry finger and roar, "You should fall down and ask God to forgive you!" Why can't we all agree that it's just as wrong to say, "What you did is fine and perhaps commendable. Just don't worry about it. Are there any other problems you'd like to talk about?"

When we find a woman is grieving over an abortion, what we should be saying is something like, "Other women have had similar problems. I *can* help you through private counseling, group counseling, and support groups. Why don't we begin by getting some more information?" Such a matter-of-fact, nonthreatening, nonintimidating approach opens the channel for communication and healing.

Jump-Starting the Grief Process

As pointed out earlier, however, the grieving process for a woman with PAS is complicated by denial. In the normal course of life, grieving immediately follows loss. In the case of PAS, however, denial may cause grieving to be delayed for months, years, or even decades. Due to the time lag, sometimes grieving won't immediately follow even when denial is broken. When this happens, it becomes necessary to "jump-start" the grieving process.[1]

You "jump-start" grieving by making certain the woman is through denial and then move her logically into a situation where it's okay to grieve. This is a necessary step in recovery for any loss. Let's suppose that instead of counseling an aborted woman, you were counseling a workman who had lost his right arm. However, as you talk to him, you notice he refers to himself as "right handed" and mentions that his "right cross" is his knockout punch. You would figure this man was in denial, right? And you can see that it is important that you get him out of it.

It does no good to yell at him. You don't have to judge him for having lost his arm. At this point, it's not even important whose fault it is that he lost his arm. You simply want him to recognize his loss so that he can process it, grieve it and go on. So you say, "Joe, I notice you keep mentioning your right arm, yet I see you've got your coat sleeve tucked into your pocket. Is there something wrong with your right arm?"

"No," he says briskly. "My right arm is just fine. I just wear my coat this way. Always have."

So you probe gently, "Describe your right arm to me."

"Well," he says, "it's like my left arm, except the thumbs are reversed—and, of course, it's stronger. And I wear my class ring on it."

His denial is strong. So you ask, "Would you do me a favor? Pick up that chair and move it over against the wall for me—and *use your right arm*." Well, the denial is strong, but not strong enough to lift a chair! So when he hesitates, you casually ask, "You had an accident a few years ago, didn't you? Was that on a Monday or a Tuesday? What kind of day was it? What happened when you got to work? What happened then?"

The example just given is, of course, patently ridiculous. I've never known a "phantom arm" to last much beyond the shock of losing it. However, the silly story does point up the importance of our previous chapter on breaking denial and how you may matter-of-factly work through denial by focusing on details. *Getting the details out and in the open "jump-starts" the grieving process.*

Treatment Tools

In the previous chapter, we discussed *diagnostic tools*, particularly the use of written and oral questionnaires. We use several treatment tools in completing the grieving process, selecting those that seem best to the woman herself. We want to promote healing with the minimum amount of trauma necessary—keeping in mind that healing inevitably involves a certain amount of pain.

Letter Writing

Letter writing is one effective treatment tool. We've had patients work through the grieving process by writing letters to boyfriends, husbands, doctors, nurses, parents and the dead baby/POC. *These letters are never mailed of course,* but writing them helps the aborted woman work through her feelings and grieve her loss.

The letters usually accomplish two purposes. The first purpose is to allow the aborted woman to recognize and express her feeling of victimization and anger. "This was all *your* fault!" "You made me do it!" "If only you had _____, then this wouldn't have happened to me!" Such accusations continue the ongoing process of breaking denial.

The second purpose of having a patient write the letters is that writing them tends to lead her to accept the event and process the feelings involved. Remember, anger is a natural part of grieving and recovery.

In most cases, letter writing also helps bring the responsibility home to the PAS woman. She sees that, while others may have had a role in the decision to abort and they might have prevented the abortion, in the final analysis, the abortion was *her* decision. In any case, what is done is done, and nothing can undo it.

Psychodrama

When the patient has trouble expressing the facts and her feelings about them, I often turn to psychodrama as a treatment tool. In my practice, I sometimes rely on standard psychodrama procedures when the woman reaches a point where she finds the abortion "just too painful to talk about."

Some patients take to psychodrama better than others. Sue Ellen, whose story I shared in chapter 1, is a good example. She had been unable to express and process the emotional turmoil she was feeling. Yet by acting out how she thought *the baby felt*, she was able to get in touch with her own feelings and continue with her grieving.

The Road Not Taken

Robert Frost's famous poem, "The Road Not Taken," points to another technique I have found valuable in facilitating the grieving process. The poem concerns a traveler who comes to a fork in the road and must decide which way to go. After evaluating the options, he makes his choice. Yet even as he begins his trip down the road of his own choosing, he admits that the way he has chosen will probably change the whole outcome of his life.

> I shall be telling this with a sigh
> Somewhere ages and ages hence:
> Two roads diverged in a wood, and I—
> I took the one less traveled by,
> *And that has made all the difference."*
> MOUNTAIN INTERVAL, 1916

Sometimes it is good to allow a patient to go back to the divergent roads in her own life and mentally walk down the *other* path—her own "road not taken"—to pretend for a moment that at each juncture, a different thing had been said and a different decision reached. When I feel she is mentally "stuck at the crossroads," thinking, "Oh, if only I had _____!" I offer her an opportunity to rewrite the drama and *let it end as she wants it to end*. Most often, we go back to the moment she entered the room where the abortion took place, but sometimes it is necessary to let her explore more lost options at all the steps along the way.

This is where the art of counseling comes into play. There are no hard and fast rules because each woman and each set of circumstances is different. She may need to act out one scenario when she talks to the counselor at the abortion center. She may want to act out a different scenario with her husband or boyfriend. She may want to change the discussion or decision in the car going to the abortion center. My role as counselor is to guide her mind, but to let her needs guide me.

Is allowing an aborted woman to live out a "what if?" fantasy a form of "enabling" her dysfunction? Certainly not! This form of psychodrama merely provides her with an opportunity to explore the feelings associated with taking a different turn in the road before proceeding to the next stage.

As an example, suppose she's hung up emotionally with the trip to the abortion center. Her boyfriend is driving and he's encouraging her to go through with the abortion. She, on the other hand, is having second thoughts. As the scene is replayed, the counselor asks what she's feeling, what she's thinking. She replies, "I'm feeling betrayed and I'm angry." The counselor asks, "What *did* you say to him?" and she replies, "I didn't say anything."

The counselor asks, "What *would you like to have said?*" She explodes, "I'd have asked, 'Why are you making me do this? You know I want the baby, and it's your baby too, why don't you want it?'" What she wanted to say isn't as important as the fact she finally got to say it.

After a woman has mentally gone down a "road not taken," she will usually fall silent. The counselor then needs to move on to the next fork in the road. "What did you do next?"

Baseball great Yogi Berra, in his inimitable manner, said "It ain't over 'til it's over." The trauma a PAS woman feels as a result of her abortion also "ain't over 'til it's over." A counselor has to make as many stops as necessary and stay at each stop until the woman is ready to move on.

Group Therapy

I always start treatment of PAS patients one-on-one. However, I try to move her into group therapy as soon as it is practical. For one thing, group treatment saves the patient money, but there are other benefits as well. There is a tie between those who have walked the same road. Counselors can understand how a PAS woman feels, but we cannot feel as she feels, because most counselors have not had the experience of having an abortion.

Another reason for group therapy is simply that grieving is not a private matter. It has a more social context, and it is really more appropriately done in a group. Grieving requires some external support and confirmation that the grief is right and acceptable. In "normal" bereavement, this external support is expressed at the hospital, at the funeral home, and at the grave site. In the delayed grieving of PAS, the support that was denied the patient at the time of the abortion can be supplied by the group.

Group counseling is also good because the intense feelings the woman with PAS feels comes out better among peers than it does one-on-one. The group not only provides sympathetic ears but mutual support and encouragement.

Phases of Recovery

Once a woman's initial denial has been broken, she has remembered the event, faced the fact that she has experienced loss, and acknowledged her responsibility. She now needs to *personalize* the experience by reliving the pregnancy, the abortion, and the aftermath of the abortion through dialogue, psychodrama, group therapy, and the other techniques mentioned above. Her treatment will usually proceed through the following phases:

Phase One: Feeling her loss
Phase Two: Reliving and processing the abortion event

Phase Three: Processing personal responsibility
Phase Four: Overcoming feelings of victimization
Phase Five: Including significant others in recovery

Phase One: Feeling the Loss

After denial has been broken initially, the aborted woman realizes:

I have lost something.
I have lost my innocence.
I have lost years or months out of my life over this problem.
I have lost relationships.
I have lost my child/potential child.

At this point, she needs to *feel* her loss, to experience her feelings of regret and sadness and then work through these feelings.

She may or may not grieve over the loss of a child or a potential child. Her sadness may be over the three or four years of dysfunction she's suffered, the relationships she's strained or severed, or the emotional problems she's endured. But whether she feels the loss of something as concrete as a child or as abstract as lost time, the feeling of loss is significant.

In my own practice, I've discovered that women with PAS invariably feel they've lost a baby. If you counsel one who doesn't, she may still be in denial, or she may genuinely feel that way. This is something that has to be worked out between counselor and counselee.

Those who do feel they've lost a child often feel grief as intense as that associated with the loss of a spouse or an older child or another significant relationship. There may be something in the chemistry between mother and developing baby/POC that creates a symbiotic relationship . . . we don't know. Whatever the scientific reason, PAS women I have worked with have felt a tremendous sense of loss as they break through denial—and they require time to grieve that loss. Because denial has been at work, even though years or even decades may have passed, the grief will be as intense and as fresh as if the abortion had taken place that very morning. Clinicians have long recognized that the hardest loss to handle is the loss of a child. The bonding between parent and child is typically much stronger than between spouses. You can *unchoose* a mate, but not a child. The old saw says, "blood is thicker than water." Blood also seems to make a thicker bond than matrimony.

Phase Two: Reliving and Processing the Abortion Event

This second phase of the grieving process for PAS takes time. You may get through only one event in a session. What the patent medicines call "speedy relief" may not be possible, but relief is. Because denial can be so strong, PAS usually takes time to manifest itself. It is reasonable to expect that recovery will also require time.

I use the questionnaires filled in during the initial interviews as "road maps" for guiding a patient through this part of the grief process. We go over each point in the questionnaire together, reliving the events. We may do two pages without a pause, then we'll get stuck somewhere and we'll stop and talk about it. We may do a paragraph of dialogue at a time or maybe only a sentence at a time. Sometimes the recollections come one word at a time. We stay until she can not only recall the experience in clear detail but she can also process it emotionally.

It is important that the abortion event be processed sequentially. Don't jump to the end or back and forth. It is the trauma of a *real event* that is giving her trouble, and the real event had a position in time. There was the time before the event, immediately before the event, the event, then the time immediately following the event and so on. It has to be processed that way.

PAS patients who have broken their initial denial have the facts about the abortion events; they merely lack emotional responses to those facts. They may be able to write down every detail, but may have difficulty telling how they *felt* at each point in the procedure. At this point, they tend to be most cooperative with their counselor, because they instinctively realize there *must be emotional reactions to these events* and that their lack of emotion signals that something is wrong.

The emotions have been suppressed or repressed because the woman has not allowed herself to think about the abortion in the past. When she started telling about the procedure in a nonthreatening atmosphere, the emotions come back to the surface.

These feelings are free to come to the surface when we:

set the stage by going back to the event

help the patient explain what did happen

use psychodrama and the "road not taken" technique to help the patient explain what *they would like to have happened instead.*

Let's put it into another context. Suppose we're counseling with a rape victim. She has suppressed this event and her feelings associated with it because the terror, horror, and anger of the event is too much for her to handle. To bring her to terms with what happened, we must bring her back to the event, no matter how reluctant she may be.

"When was it?"

"It was January 31, 1989. I had been working late, and when I got to my car, he came up behind me and. . . ."

"What happened?"

"He made me drive him to the park, then. . . ."

"What did you do?"

"I lay there. I didn't move. Didn't say a word. Scared to death he was going to kill me."

"What would you have *liked to have happened?*"

A typical response is, "I wish I'd put a pistol in my purse and blown his brains out!"

So we matter-of-factly say, "Let's go back and redo what you wanted to do using psychodrama."

The key is to keep piecing the event together until both the memory of the event and her feelings about it are clear. If you stop short, then the healing process is short-circuited and she will be frustrated, confused and may lapse back into denial.

It may sound somewhat cruel and inhumane to cause a person to relive a stressful event that has caused her pain for months or even years. Yet counselors, like dentists, sometimes must use methods that cause intense short-term pain in order to alleviate chronic pain.

When Dorothy Bockmon was a child on an East Texas farm in the thirties, it was fashionable among farm folk to have bobtailed dogs. Dorothy and the other eight kids in the family decided it was time to bring their dog up in the fashion world. So they borrowed a sharp knife from the kitchen and, without a word to anyone, took the dog out in the field for his operation.

The dog, who was about three years old at this point, willingly followed, not knowing what was in store. So they sat him on a stump and while some kids petted him, others stretched out his thick yellow tail and yet another took the knife in hand to do the deed. However, the kids loved the dog, so instead of chopping off the tail in one fell swoop, they just cut it a little until he yelped. Then they petted and soothed him until he relaxed a bit, then they cut it a little deeper. The poor dog suffered all afternoon for what would have been a two-second operation if they'd grabbed the dog by the tail and gotten the unpleasant operation over with.

The kindest thing we can do is to help the patient get through the unpleasantness so she can get on with life. If we stop short of what needs to be done because of our empathy for her pain, then we are unnecessarily prolonging the treatment and postponing the recovery process.

The kindest way to come to terms with delayed grieving is to come to grips with the events and get it done.

The sequence for processing the abortion event is:

1. Have her write down the event in the best detail she can.
2. Have her verbally work through the feelings associated with each step of the event until she runs out of detail.
3. Have her progress until she's past the most stressful point.
4. Once you've dealt with the actual abortion, proceed to the events immediately following the procedure.

Phase Three: Processing Personal Responsibility

As we move forward in sequence from the decision to the abortion itself, I usually find there's a growing sense of significant loss on the part of the PAS patient. This is true regardless of the euphemistic language she may have used heretofore. Just as the process of breaking denial continues gradually throughout grieving, so do the various phases. Thus the phase of feeling sadness over loss continues on a deeper level through the process of reliving events.

I was counseling with one woman who consistently referred to the aborted item as a *product of conception*. She was telling about the trip to the abortion center, and I asked, "What did you and your boyfriend talk about in the car as you were driving to the abortion center?"

She said, "I told him I didn't want to do it."

"Do what?" I asked.

She thought a long moment, then began weeping. "I told him I didn't want to kill my baby," she sobbed.

For the first time, she admitted that *although she had used the proper depersonalized abortion language, she hadn't really bought into it*. Now, why was that admission important? Because, as I have pointed out earlier, *no one grieves the loss of tissue*. If she had been convinced she had simply removed a "mass of cells," then that would have been fine with me—only then she wouldn't have been suffering from postabortion syndrome! When she admitted her true feelings, she was breaking denial and beginning to work her way through grief.

As usual, I made no comment about the use of the noun *baby*, but from that point on, that's the way she referred to what had been aborted. She went from the impersonal medical language to traditional language, which was appropriate, because grieving is intensely personal.

It is said the six hardest words to say are, "I admit I made a mistake." Whatever abortion may be to other women, to the woman with PAS, the abortion was a mistake. Once she's out of denial, even though she's acknowledged that she is responsible for her act, she is still likely to feel she's "been had," to feel that she has been victimized. This may be true, to a certain extent, but in most cases it is a cop-out, another way of to avoid accepting personal responsibility. "My boyfriend/husband *made me do it!*" "The abortion counselor *made me* do it." "It's not my fault."

As I've indicated throughout this book, this is nothing new. In the Genesis account of creation, Eve tried to absolve herself of responsibility by saying, "The serpent (devil) made me do it." Adam's freely translated response to God was, "The woman *you* gave me was obviously defective and she made me do it. Therefore, it's mostly her fault and ultimately the fault is yours." The tendency to blame someone else for our misfortunes is human, is natural, is understandable. Yet there can be no real healing until we fully accept *personal responsibility* for our actions.

Once we have broken denial, once we have grieved the loss, the next question is, "how did this happen?" The PAS woman must come to terms with reality:

1. I got pregnant.
2. I decided to have an abortion.
3. I gave an abortionist some money.

4. The abortionist did what I wanted.
5. If it was a baby that was killed, I'm the one who killed it.

Number five looks stark and harsh. I can hear a rousing chorus of objections from those with a strong pro-abortion/pro-choice stance. Put away the tar and feathers for a moment and let's examine the issue.

"What happened to your clinical objectivity?" you ask.

It's a good question. The answer is, the clinical objectivity is still there. Remember we agreed that helping the PAS woman was so important that *we had to set aside our own preconceived notions and ideas.* That means we have to call things what she calls them. I have never worked with a woman suffering from PAS who felt she'd removed a "product of conception." In her mind, she killed her baby, otherwise she'd have no more emotional problem than if she had a wart removed. Okay, if that's what happened, and if she's the one who made it happen, then the responsibility is hers. If a woman at this point is distraught and grieving and still wants to call it a *product of conception,* then our responsibility is to help her grieve the loss of the POC. But I'm convinced it won't happen in your practice any more than it happens in mine.

A lot of women have worked their way through to intellectually acknowledge "a baby died in the abortion" without fully accepting personal responsibility for the steps leading up to that death. Just acknowledging personal responsibility in the outcome *alone* may bring some measure of emotional relief, but it stops short of a full recovery. Until a woman with PAS can accept that she purchased the service that caused the stress that brought on PAS, she won't get well—or at least her healing won't be complete. Stopping short of a full realization and acceptance of what occurred and why will keep her from processing the full measure of grief. And she is going to stay unwell until she has completed that grieving process.

Phase Four: Overcoming Feelings of Victimization

In an earlier chapter, we discussed the fact that many aborted women feel a sense of victimization. Processing personal responsibility means she realizes that while she may have been a victim of the system, the decision was nevertheless hers. This does not mean, however, that the system is automatically absolved of all responsibility, but that she must honestly and courageously face the part she played and grieve over her mistakes.

Once she has done this, however, the next phase involves coming to terms with her feelings of victimization and consciously giving up the victim's role. This means placing a fair share of the blame *back* on those who share responsibility with her and expressing her feelings of anger and powerlessness.

When it comes to working through feelings of victimization, I find that most women in PAS don't blame the abortion ads or the *counselor* who made the arrangements at the abortion center. Instead, they blame the physician who performed the service. In group psychodrama, I've had women lying on the floor with their legs spread, "talking" to the doctor's head. (Since they are usually draped, that's all they see of him.) They talk right through their legs at him, and most of them want to kick him right in the face. Since their legs are strapped in the stirrups, no one ever has, but they fantasize about it.

(I'm not faulting physicians for using stirrups and straps. They have to restrain the patient because any sudden movement could cause complications. However, the woman's feelings of helplessness and resentment are also understandable. In any event, while facts may be right or wrong, feelings are neither.)

The anger they feel as they relive those moments at this point is entirely different from the anger they may have felt during the *victimization* stage. They are now past those feelings and this anger is directed toward building a sense of control over their lives.

This is a good stage of therapy. It's wholesome and healthy, and it lets the group and the woman involved know that they've rounded the bend and that the storms and gales and rocks and reefs are behind them. They're in sight of home, because now that can act out one last "road not taken" and even laugh a bit thinking how startled the doctor would have been if he'd been knocked for a loop.

Phase Five: Including Significant Others in Recovery

The first four phases of the grieving process for PAS occur more or less naturally, following sequentially once denial is broken. The fifth, though vital to recovery, may require much encouragement on the part of the counselor. The PAS sufferer must reach out to the "significant others," those who have suffered as a result of her PAS. These may include a husband, a boyfriend, siblings, parents, and/or her closest personal friends.

In most cases I've treated, the abortion has been either a secret *from* the family and close friends or a *family* secret. Because others have not known *why the woman with PAS has changed,* they have been unable to understand mood, personality, and lifestyle changes. This is why it is important that the secret be shared once the PAS patient has sufficiently recovered from her own grief. We're not talking about a *True Confession* scenario, but about sharing enough of the turmoil to explain the behavior. Relationships can't be built on false, misleading, or insufficient data, and damaged relationships can't be repaired with silence or misinformation. Restoration requires an attitude of honesty, which necessitates at least partial disclosure of the reason for the change in behavior.

Many times, family members know *something* happened to their daughter or sister—they just don't know *what.* Knowing what has happened will give them the framework to build understanding. Other times, family members will have learned from other sources about the abortion but, since it was never mentioned by the aborted woman, they never talked about it. Once the aborted woman broaches the subject, conversation and healing can flow. True, now there is a grieving *family* instead of just a grieving *individual*—but chances are the family was grieving anyway because of the unexplained changes they saw in the PAS patient. Besides, grieving is usually best handled in a supportive family context.

After the PAS patient has dealt with her abortion, I don't just tell them, "Go home and tell your family all about it and have a nice day." Usually, I handle the "how to" in a group training session. However, there are sometimes special circumstances when I am more directly involved. This is what happened in the case of Linda.

Case History: Linda

In February of 1986, I was a guest on the Focus on the Family radio program. This program, hosted by psychologist James Dobson, is heard by millions of people coast to coast. The topic was the aftereffects of abortion. Joining us in the broadcast were three women who had suffered emotional problems as a result of their abortions. As we discussed the pain and suffering that often follows an abortion, the switchboard was flooded with calls, and more than ten thousand people wrote in for information. Right after we went off the air, I got a call from a young lady I'll call Linda.

Linda told me she had had an abortion twelve years earlier and it had totally ruined her life. She also told me that she had been preparing to commit suicide when she happened to turn across the radio dial and caught the program. As if to show her seriousness about suicide, she shared that she had closed out her bank account and quit her job. Her apartment lease expired the next day, and she intended to be moved out dead.

As we continued to talk, I learned that Linda had been raised a Roman Catholic and that her whole family was active in pro-life causes in a midwestern state. Her father was a physician who was personally and professionally opposed to artificial methods of birth control. When she had become pregnant in school, she hadn't been able to bring herself to tell her family or face the responsibility, so she had gotten an abortion. For twelve years she'd tried to escape the pain of that deed, losing herself in work, drugs, and alcohol. "Now," she said, "unless you *know* you can help me, I'm ready to end it all." Think counselors don't have pressure in their work? I quickly shared my conviction that there is help, there is hope, and there is recovery—but that it was unreasonable to expect twelve years of problems to be solved in a single phone call. I asked what city she lived in, and was delighted to find that she did not live far from me. After eliciting her promise to do nothing until we talked, we made an appointment for the following week. Needless to say, I was praying that she *would* show up, because her discussion of suicide had been so matter-of fact, her preparations so complete, that there was no way to doubt her seriousness.

Linda did show up for her appointment. She looked tired, listless, and a decade older than her thirty-three years. After the preliminaries were over, she went to the heart of the matter.

At age twenty-one, she had gone to a counselor for help with an emotional problem. The counselor, a discredit to his profession, had betrayed her trust, taken advantage of her naiveté, and turned the counseling sessions into sexual encounters. When she became pregnant, he had arranged for the abortion and accompanied her into the abortion room to make certain it was done. After that, he had wanted nothing else to do with her.

Linda had been devastated by what had happened. Not only had she broken her own moral code regarding premarital sex, she had been taken advantage of by someone who was supposed to help solve her problems, not help create them.

She then decided, on her own, to make whatever atonement she could for what she had done. She studied developmental psychology and, upon graduation, began working with *profoundly* retarded people. To understand the degree of her penance and the amount of pressure she operated under, you have to understand that these people had IQ's below 25, and they would never advance beyond the mental age of an infant or toddler. Most needed constant care to survive, and only a few would ever learn to recognize even familiar faces.

The work Linda chose was important and needed to be done. However, it was a tough, thankless task; the highlight of her day would not be teaching someone to feed himself, but having him bite down on a spoon at the proper time. Due to the high frustration level of this kind of work, the typical worker burns out after eighteen to twenty-four months. *Linda had been working sixty-hour weeks for twelve years!* As Linda continued her sessions with me, working her way through the steps of grieving, the big question in her mind was how she would tell her parents. Considering her father's prominent pro-life/anti-abortion stand and his high lay position within the Catholic church, I agreed that this was one time when the counselor needed to be there to help everyone deal with the problem.

Linda called her parents and asked them to come to our offices and not ask questions before they got there. This was difficult for the family, but they followed her instructions. After all, as her mother said, "She has been very disturbed for twelve years, and now she's acting normally again." Linda shared the entire story with her family, and even though they were terribly hurt, *at least they understood what Linda had been going through.* And like families everywhere, they surrounded her with their love. They were supportive and forgiving. They were glad the secret was out and they wanted to help her get on with her life. There was no condemnation, no sense of betrayal—only love and care and concern.

Interestingly enough, Linda's father dropped off two thousand dollars on the way out to pay for her therapy. It wasn't asked for, it wasn't necessary, but he insisted. He said he could afford it, and it was worth ten times that much to have his daughter back.

Incidentally, wrapping up Linda's case involved more than just involving her family. For while many post-aborted women *feel* victimized, Linda really *was* a victim of the counselor who seduced her. She wanted to make certain that no other unsuspecting girl ever went through what she experienced. So she wrote the counselor's licensure board. It turned out that hers was not the only complaint, and this unscrupulous man was forced from the profession. Taking action helped her overcome her feeling of victimization and, in so doing, she regained her pride. She felt she had cleansed herself by her action and her recovery after that point was swift.

Most Families Are Supportive

Almost invariably, I have found that families are supportive of women with PAS once they understand the situation. Oh, they may feel crushed beyond words; the abortion may have flown in the face of everything they hold near and dear. But when it comes down to forgiveness, families forgive if they know what they're forgiving. For all the talk about the demise of the nuclear family, the family tie is still the tie that binds people together and binds up wounds. After all, the family has seen the *before* and they've seen the *after*. At this point, what they're really concerned about is the *ever after*.

I've talked to many younger girls with PAS who had an abortion because they couldn't bear to hurt their parents. But when they developed PAS, their destructive lifestyles hurt their parents far more than they would have been hurt by a problem pregnancy. When parents see their daughters restored after treatment, they are almost invariably forgiving and supportive.

Sometimes parents are supportive not only of their own child, but of the other child involved as well. Just the other night, I received a call from a man in northern Illinois. He had heard me on a radio show somewhere and had not only tracked me down, but obtained my home number. He told me, "I'm a Christian and we're a Christian family. My son got a girl pregnant, and that's not good, but that's a fact. My son's not happy about this, and the girl's not happy about this, and neither family is happy. Yet we want to handle it from *what we see* as a Christian perspective.

"We want the baby to be born, but the girl's mother has convinced her to have an abortion. We have discussed it with her. We have pleaded with her. We have begged her not to abort the baby. We've told her that we'll pay all the expenses and they can keep the baby and put it up for adoption, or we'll take the baby and raise it ourselves. We will do anything that is necessary.

"My son is absolutely devastated by this. He is an emotional wreck, he loves the girl and doesn't want her to have the abortion. They're both sophomores in high school. Yet they're going to Chicago and have the abortion tomorrow. What can we do?"

I explained to the man on the phone that if a pregnant woman wants to carry a child and the father doesn't, the father is still legally liable for that child's welfare until that child is of age. However, if the mother doesn't want to carry the child, the father had no legal rights whatsoever.

He sobbed on the phone and I held the receiver while he shared the news with his family. He came back a moment later and asked, "Isn't there *anything* we can do to stop this abortion?"

I hesitated a moment and said, "This sounds like pride on the part of the girl's mother. I've heard of some cases where, if enough money changed hands, an irate mother was could be persuaded to let her daughter carry to term."

He said they weren't wealthy people and that the girl's mother had already called the sheriff and said she didn't want anyone from his family contacting them again. The best I could do was refer their family to a competent counselor in their own area. He thanked me and hung up. I never heard from him again. This story, in addition to showing how families can be supportive, also shows that *men* as well as women can be deeply affected by an abortion. True, since PAS comes about as a result of trauma related to a real event that happens to women, the vast majority of sufferers are women. However, men can and do suffer from PAS as well. It isn't as severe, because there is no physical involvement beyond the initial intercourse—no symbiotic relationship during pregnancy, no pain during abortion. But it does happen. I have heard many such stories from the biological fathers of aborted babies and dads who were devastated by abortion.

Case History: Helen

As I have indicated, reaching out to significant others—especially family—is far easier than the PAS suffer usually imagines. But even when this is not true, as in Helen's case, the act of sharing with significant others is important to the healing process.

Helen came from a religious background. Her father was a pastor who ran an evangelical Bible camp. When she was fifteen, she got pregnant, and her parents insisted that she have an abortion because her pregnancy would ruin her father's ministry.

Helen had slipped from her church's high moral standard, but she insisted she would not violate her church's stand on abortion. "Two wrongs don't make a right," she argued. "I'll give the baby up for adoption, but I must carry the baby."

So her parents tricked her. They said, "Okay, if you insist on having the baby, we'll stand with you. But we have to take you to Dr. _____ for an examination to make certain everything is all right." So they got her down to the doctor, who had her lie down on the examining table and strapped her legs into the stirrups. By this time, Helen knew she had been betrayed and began squirming and screaming and pleading, but neither the parents nor doctor were in the least affected. They performed a forced abortion, gave her a stern lecture about future behavior, and that was that.

Except it wasn't. From that point on, Helen couldn't stand her parents. They didn't practice what they preached, so she reasoned that what they preached must not be very important, either. Her one indiscretion became a whole series. She jumped on the "free love" bandwagon of the early 1970s and actively tried to see how many people she could have sex with. Soon she was pregnant again, and this time she went back to the same physician and purchased her own abortion.

Eventually, Helen sensed that her behavior was self-destructive. She felt there had to be more out of life. So she tried to get well on her own. She got married, started going to church again, and attempted to lead a normal life.

Then Helen got pregnant. She was ecstatic. This child was to be a replacement for the ones she had lost, particularly the one that had been taken from her. Then, in her sixth month, she went into labor. The baby was born dead.

Helen was devastated. She felt certain God was punishing her for the abortions. She got pregnant again, and after a fretful, worry-fraught pregnancy, delivered a healthy baby. She relaxed. She felt at peace. In her mind, the healthy baby was a sign that God had forgiven her.

Eighteen months later, Helen became pregnant again, and this time she enjoyed her pregnancy. Once again, she delivered a healthy, happy baby. But when this baby was ten months old, she left it with a sitter and went out for a few hours. When she came back, the baby was dead, a victim of sudden infant death syndrome (SIDS), popularly called "crib death."

Now Helen was absolutely suicidal. She felt this tragedy was a punishment for the second baby she had aborted—now she and God were even, two for two. And she feared her other child might have to die at any moment. She went into such deep depression that she had to be hospitalized. She wanted to die, she said, "I can't stay here to kill another child! I've killed four now!"

When I first saw Helen, she was what the general public would call a "basket case." She was subject to uncontrollable crying during the day and nightmares at night. She had to be hospitalized repeatedly, and they wanted to medicate her, and she didn't want to be medicated. She wanted to be left alone so she could die.

At church, Helen heard talk about forgiveness. She was assured that God was a loving Father who loved her and would never punish someone who repented, no matter what they had done. Yet she wasn't sure she could buy that. Her spiritual experience indicated that God was a stern Father who punished severely. "After all," she reasoned, "My father is a pastor, and he hurt me. My "heavenly Father" must be like him. My earthly father killed one of my children, and my heavenly Father killed two."

We began, of course, at the beginning. It was relatively easy to convince Helen that the first abortion was *not her fault*. She was no more to blame than a rape victim; she had been tricked, and she had been medically assaulted. She worked through her guilt feelings over that one quickly and well. She missed the baby, but she saw she had no responsibility for what happened.

The guilt feelings over the second abortion were more intense. But by following the steps outlined in previous chapters, she was able to come to grips with that as well. Then we went through the miscarriage and the crib death.

Today, Helen no longer suffers from depression and is fully recovered. She has a loving and supportive husband and a beautiful, healthy child. Although she has shared all her feelings with her parents, to my knowledge neither of them have ever expressed remorse for what they did. They felt the ministry was the most important thing, and that's the way they acted. Nevertheless, the process of reaching out to them was important to Helen's recovery.

Forgiveness Is Required

Part of the process of reaching out to others is forgiveness. The woman must forgive those she feels failed her or deserted her or victimized her. Then she must forgive herself. Forgiveness is never easy—and the deeper the hurt, the more disfiguring the scars, the more difficult it becomes. This is an area where faith, which is covered in the following chapter, plays an important role.

8

The Importance of Faith

Most of us are religious people. A recent Gallup poll says that nearly 90 percent of Americans claim to believe in a personal God. Under the circumstances, it would be illogical to leave God out of the grieving and healing processes.

For reasons that are not always clear, the media and the medical and mental health professions as a whole have tended to ignore the spiritual aspect of our lives as if it weren't important. In fact, some "experts" have said that our religious beliefs *themselves* have *caused* many of our physical and emotional problems because these beliefs contribute to *guilt*. To that charge, people of faith respond, "We feel guilty because we *are guilty.*"

Dr. Karl Menninger, founder of the Menninger Clinic and Foundation in Topeka, Kansas, has been a driving force for improved psychiatric care. He wrote a classic volume on humanity's flight from guilt titled, *Whatever Became of Sin?* (New York: E. P. Dutton, 1978). In this book he demonstrates the universality of guilt—and the justification for it. He recites an incident in which a stern-faced

119

man stood on the street corner in the busy Chicago Loop. As pedestrians hurried by, this man would solemnly lift his right arm and, pointing to the person nearest him, intone the single word, "GUILTY!"

Menninger writes:

> The effect of this strange j'accuse pantomime on the passing strangers was extraordinary, almost eerie. They would stare at him, hesitate, look away, look at each other, and then at him again; then hurriedly continue on their ways.
>
> One man, turning to another who was my informant, exclaimed: "But how did he know?"
>
> No doubt many others had similar thoughts. How did he know, indeed?
>
> "Guilty!" Everyone guilty? Guilty of what? Guilty of overparking? Guilty of lying? Guilty of arrogance and hubris toward the one God? Guilty of borrowing, not to say embezzling? Guilty of unfaithfulness to a faithful wife? Guilty of evil thoughts—or evil plans?
>
> Guilty before whom? Is a police officer following? Did anyone see? Will they be likely to notice it? Does he know about it? But that isn't technically illegal, is it?
>
> I can make it up. I will give it back. I'll apologize. I wasn't myself when I did that. No one knows about it. But I'm going to quit. It's a dangerous habit. I wouldn't want the children to see me. How can I ever straighten it out? What's done can't be undone.

Dr. Menninger continues:

> The solemn accuser on the Chicago street corner has had many predecessors. In the eighth to sixth centuries B.C., peripatetic exhorters held forth in thriving Palestinian villages attracting large and attentive crowds. To their listeners these earnest young men likewise cried "guilty" and proclaimed ominously that for all the general prosperity, sin was prevalent thereabouts which, unacknowledged and unrepented, would bring dire consequences. These men were ignored, ridiculed as alarmists, jailed as trespassers, or driven from the country. In the course of time, their predictions were fulfilled and their countries were annihilated.

After a brief trip through history, Dr. Menninger says of our own time and its tendency to ignore the spiritual element in life: "Suddenly we awoke from our pleasant dreams with a fearful realization that *something was wrong.*" Indeed, something was and is wrong. When we remove the religious underpinnings from our lives, those lives tend to fall apart. Even when we tell ourselves we are not guilty—we still *feel* guilty. The rantings of a *fundamentalist?* Perhaps, but they are echoed by secular historians Will and Ariel Durant. In their book, *The Story of Civilization* (New York: Simon and Schuster, 1935), they write, "We shall find it no easy task to mold a natural ethic strong enough to maintain moral restraint and social order without the support of supernatural consolations, hopes and fears. . . . There is not a significant example in history, before our time, of a society successfully maintaining a moral life without the aid of religion."

What has been the sum total of the modern trend to view our historic "freedom *of* religion" as "freedom *from* religion?" Perhaps the best way to arrive at the clearest answer is to go back in time to the earliest months of this decade, when Ronald Reagan was challenging incumbent Jimmy Carter for the presidency. At the time, the inflation rate was 15 percent and interest rates were more than 20 percent and unemployment was rising rapidly. And in this context, candidate Reagan asked the question that clinched his election. He said, in effect, "Look back at the country four years ago and ask yourself, 'Am I better off today than I was four years ago?' If the answer is 'yes,' then vote for my opponent. If the answer is 'no,' vote for me."

As we look at the issues that are tearing our country apart, *those of us old enough to remember* might ask ourselves "Are we better off in what many call the "post Christian age" than we were when prayer was in schools and sex education was not? Are we better off without a Hollywood moral code than we were with one? Are our children better off for having access to R and X movies and videos than we were when everything was rated G? Are we better off with today's acceptance of pornography than we were when possession of same was a quick ticket to jail? Are we better off with today's "enlightened" and liberal abortion laws than we were with the more restrictive laws of the past? Each of us must answer those questions for ourselves, and we must communicate our answers to those who make policy decisions. The face and fate of America hinges on how we answer.

Menninger asked, "Whatever became of sin?" Is sin an archaic concept that belongs only in churches and synagogues (if it belongs anywhere at all)? It would seem that the concept of sin has changed in America today . . . but that the historic "wages of sin" have not.

This much is certain, when we violate our own faith, our own moral code, we must be prepared to pay the psychological consequences. For every action, there is a separate but equal reaction. This is illustrated in the case of Jessie.

Case History: Jessie

When Jessie was nineteen, she had everything going for her. She was attending a religious college in a midwestern state and her father was a prosperous banker. Her family was very active and not only worshiped together each Sunday, but worshiped as a family *daily*. Then she met this boy and it was—or seemed to be—love at first sight. Jessie was one of those women that usually exist only in movies: she got pregnant the very first time she had sex. She knew of one girl on campus who had gotten pregnant and she had been asked to leave college. Jessie didn't want to leave college, so without saying a word to her boyfriend or her parents, she went to a doctor's office and had a dilation and curettage (D&C) uterine abortion.

Eight years later, Jessie came to see me. She was alcoholic and drug dependent, had been divorced once, and was in the final stages of a second divorce. (She had two children.) Once she was diagnosed with PAS, I asked her about the abortion. She said, "It was like this. I was a good

Lutheran girl, on a Lutheran campus, and if they found out I was not married and pregnant, they'd kick me out. I didn't want to leave school, so I had the abortion."

In Jessie's case, the abortion itself wasn't a particularly painful event. Oh, she had some pain during the abortion, but nothing beyond her ability to cope, and she had no medical problems afterwards. Her pain was emotional, because she was convinced that she had "taken a human life" and, moreover, that she had done it for her own convenience—so she could stay in school.

She couldn't handle that kind of trauma. She broke up with the boyfriend, who had never even known she was pregnant. (It is not unusual for a woman to find she's pregnant, have an abortion, and never tell the man who impregnated her. It seems to be the feminine version of the double standard, "It's a woman's problem, I'll have to take care of it myself.) She turned to alcohol and drugs to ease the emotional pain. She quit school—bringing on herself the very punishment she had chosen an abortion to avoid.

Often, PAS is delayed due to denial. In Jessie's case, she walked out of the abortion clinic suffering from post-abortion syndrome because she never denied what she was doing or doubted that it was wrong. As she told me, "I knew when I went in that I would be taking my baby's life."

I asked, "Jessie, in your mind, was it a fetus?"

Without a moment's hesitation, she replied, "No, no—it was a baby. It was a baby. We don't have to go through that. I knew what I was doing. I told them I knew what I was doing. I went into the abortion room, and they started the machines up. They stuck their instruments up inside me, and they scraped my baby out and threw it away in a big stainless-steel sink with a garbage disposer in it.

"As soon as it was over, I felt different. They were cleaning me up and I lifted the sheet and looked down. My breasts had already gotten smaller. My body already knew I'd never nurse that baby.

"I'd thought I'd known what I was doing before then.

All of a sudden it *really dawned on me what I had done!* Killing my baby wasn't just an intellectual decision. I suddenly realized that I was connected to that baby, just as that baby had been connected to me. The baby was dependent on me, and I had broken the connection. It was done and there was no undoing it."

The thought was too painful, so Jessie had pushed it out of her mind. Her denial developed *after* the event and carried her into a lifestyle that was destroying her. She began to get better only as she went back and faced the experience, reliving it and grieving her loss. She forgave herself, asked the baby to forgive her, asked Christ to forgive her and found help and healing in her faith.

The Power of Faith for Healing

If faith's only function was to restrain us from excesses that harm us, it would be of value. But nearly nine out of ten Americans know it has value beyond encouraging moderation and morality. It also has power to bring about healing through love and acceptance and forgiveness.

Therefore, while it is becoming more or less standard operating procedure to leave any talk of religious values out of the medical or mental-health fields, it is impossible for any counselor involved in treating the whole person not to take the religious feelings of the patient into consideration. While a counselor should not try to *convert* the counselee to his or her own personal religious view, it is natural and often necessary to encourage patients to draw on whatever comfort and strength their beliefs offer.

No less an authority than Karl Menninger in *Whatever Became of Sin,* says, "The impression prevails that moral counsel is something about which even doctors no longer concern themselves. . . . The doctor must express his opinion based on his convictions, but his specific *advice* will take into consideration his patient's convictions as well." When we are dealing with grief and loss, it is natural to draw comfort and wisdom from our own religious beliefs.

And it is routine practice in many counseling offices to refer patients with a religious preference to a priest, rabbi, or minister of their choice in the case of "normal" bereavement. It is equally important that, *at the proper time,* we encourage the woman with PAS to contact her spiritual advisor to help her come to grips with her loss through her faith.

Some women are open to and have been helped by symbolic actions such as burial or memorial services and, often, a willing minister can be found who will officiate. Virtually all who have spiritual roots are helped by relying on the same faith that sustains them through other loss. When this is done *in the proper sequence,* I've seen it bring help and healing. If the faith she has teaches forgiveness, then forgiveness is certainly what a woman who has been tormented by guilt needs.

The realist teaches "you can't unscramble an egg." Poets say, "Hearts and fine china are easily broken and never well mended." The stoic says, "Don't cry over spilt milk." But those of us who name the name of Christ know that God will forgive us—and that we must forgive ourselves. Then, having receiving forgiveness, we must "go and sin no more."

Once the woman has gone through the proper steps in grieving, *I believe a vital part of the healing process is to move the event from the physical world to the spiritual.* I believe we should let the client leave the abortion experience in the hands of a loving God and get on with her life. This means putting the past behind and pressing on with new interests and new lives. With denial broken and the grieving process concluded, and with her spiritual commitment made, she can get on with life and look forward to better days ahead.

I can't help but agree with Dr. Menninger:

> Neither theologian nor prophet nor sociologist, I am a doctor, speaking the medical tongue with a psychiatric accent. For doctors, health is the ultimate good, the ideal

state of being. And mental health—some of us believe—includes all the healths: physical, social, cultural, and moral (spiritual). To live, to love, to care, to enjoy, to build on the foundations of our predecessors, to revere the constant miracles of creation and endurance, of "the starry skies above and the moral law within"—these are acts and attitudes which express our mental health."

In World War II, when the Nazi's invaded Holland, Casper ten Boom and his two unmarried daughters, Betsie and Corrie, made the brave decision to hide Jews, knowing their act would mean imprisonment and perhaps death for them if they were discovered. Corrie asked her father what they would do if they were caught, and Casper said, "Corrie, there is no pit so deep that the love of God is not deeper still!"

Whatever your patient has done, we are convinced there is no pit so deep that God's love is not deeper still. With clinical counsel and spiritual guidance, postabortion syndrome is a treatable malady. We need to assure her

There is help.
There is hope.
There is recovery.

Appendix A

Symptoms of Post-traumatic Stress Disorder (PTSD)[1]

A. The person has experienced an event that is outside the range of usual human experience and that would be markedly distressing to almost anyone. e.g., serious threat to one's life or physical integrity; serious threat or harm to one's children, spouse, or other close relatives and friends; sudden destruction of one's home or community; or seeing another person who has recently been, or is being, seriously injured or killed as the result of an accident or physical violence.

B. The traumatic event is persistently reexperienced in at least one of the following ways:

(1) recurrent and intrusive distressing recollections of the event

(2) recurrent distressing dreams of the event

(3) sudden acting or feeling as if the traumatic event were recurring (includes a sense of reliving the experience, illusions, hallucinations, and dissociative [flashback] episodes, then those that occur upon awakening or when intoxicated)

(4) intense psychological distress at exposure to events that symbolize or resemble an aspect of the traumatic event, including anniversaries of the trauma

C. Persistent avoidance of stimuli associated with the trauma or numbing of general responsiveness (not present before the trauma), as indicated by at least three of the following:

(1) efforts to avoid thoughts or feelings associated with the trauma

(2) efforts to avoid activities or situations that arouse recollections of the trauma.

(3) inability to recall an important aspect of the trauma (psychogenic amnesia)

(4) markedly diminished interest in significant activities

(5) feeling of detachment or estrangement from others

(6) restricted range of affect, e.g., unable to have loving feelings

(7) sense of a foreshortened future, e.g., does not expect to have a career, marriage, or children, or a long life

D. Persistent symptoms of increased arousal (not present before the trauma), as indicated by at least two of the following:

(1) difficulty falling or staying asleep

(2) irritability or outbursts of anger

(3) difficulty concentrating

(4) hypervigilance

(5) exaggerated startle response (physiologic reactivity upon exposure to events that symbolize or resemble an aspect of the traumatic event e.g., a woman who was raped in an elevator breaks out in a sweat when entering any elevator)

E. Duration of the disturbance (symptoms in B, C, and D) of at least one month.

Specify delayed onset if the onset of symptoms was at least six months after the trauma.

Appendix B

Diagnostic Criteria for Postabortion Syndrome[1]

A. **Stressor:** The abortion experience, that is, the intentional destruction of a woman's unborn baby/POC, is sufficiently traumatic to cause significant symptoms of re-experience and avoidance in some women who have experienced this procedure.

B. **Re-experience** of the abortion stressor may occur in at least one of the following modes:

(1) recurrent and intrusive recollections of the abortion or the potential infant

(2) recurrent dreams of the abortion or potential child

(3) sudden acting or feeling as if the abortion were reoccurring

C. **Avoidance** phenomena by which there is reduced responsiveness or involvement with the external world may occur in at least one of the following modes:

(1) markedly diminished interest in significant activities

(2) a feeling of detachment or estrangement from others

(3) reduced capacity for feeling or expressing emotions

(4) reduced communication and/or increased hostile interactions

(5) depressed mood

D. **Associated Symptoms** include at least two of the following:

(1) hyperalertness, exaggerated startle reaction, or explosive hostile outbursts

(2) sleep disturbance

(3) intensification of symptoms by exposure to reminders of the stressor, for example, contact with pregnant mothers, nurseries, or clinics

(4) guilt about surviving when the unborn child did not or about the abortion decision, and the inability to forgive self for involvement

(5) memory impairment or trouble concentrating

(6) avoidance of activities which are reminders of the abortion stressor

E. **Subtypes** include:

(1) Acute: onset within six months of the abortion stressor and of less than six months' duration

(2) Chronic: duration longer than six months

(3) Delayed: onset more than six months after the abortion stressor[2]

Appendix C

Common Abortion Procedures[1]

Theorem: The likelihood of a woman developing PAS increases in direct proportion to the trauma of the abortion event.

A. Suction Curettage (legally performed up to twelfth week[2]):
The canal of the uterine cervix is mechanically dilated until the opening is large enough to allow the passage of a tube into the uterine cavity. The baby/POC and placenta are sucked out by means of a powerful vacuum pump attached to the inserted tube. The uterus is then examined to ensure complete removal of the baby/POC.

B. Dilation and Curettage (performed up to twelfth week):
The cervix is mechanically dilated, and the baby/POC is scraped out of the uterus with a sharp curette, which resembles a small spoon.

C. Dilation and Evacuation (performed after twelfth week):
The cervix is mechanically dilated, and the membranes and baby/POC is dismembered inside the womb and then removed with forceps.

D. Saline Abortion (performed after twelfth to fourteenth week):
Amniotic fluid is removed through the abdominal wall. This fluid is replaced with a concentrated saline solution that induces labor and results in the expulsion of a dead baby/POC within twenty-four to forty-eight hours. (Occasionally the baby/POC, though badly burned by the salt solution, has been born alive and in agony, sometimes causing severe trauma for the woman.)

E. Prostaglandin injection (performed after twelfth to fourteenth week):
A type of prostaglandin that causes strong muscular contraction is injected in milligram doses into the uterine cavity without withdrawing the amniotic fluid. The period between injection and expulsion of the baby/POC is of a shorter duration than with saline solution.

131

Appendix D

Questions and Answers About PAS

I've spoken about PAS to many professional and lay groups. After each presentation, we always try to have fifteen or twenty minutes for questions and answers. These are the questions I'm asked most often and the answers I give.

Can men get PAS?

Yes, men can and do get PAS. However, since there is no physical trauma, it is much less common and less severe. I am currently preparing a research paper on men and PAS.

You talk about the importance of religious belief as a final step in healing. What if the PAS patient has no religious background.

If you get the one in ten who doesn't believe in a personal God, then there's a 90 percent chance she believes in *some sort of supreme being.* If you do get the rare one who has no religious beliefs at all, then ask her where she thinks the baby is and suggest she leave it there and focus on the future.

Who can counsel PAS women?

Lay counselors can provide support within the normal context of friendship. More in-depth counseling requires professional training and skills.

When should there be a referral to a professional?

When the aborted woman is having an emotional, psychological, relational, or spiritual problem directly related to the abortion itself, she should be referred.

How many women have PAS?

We don't know. The record keeping systems for abortion procedures are not as adequate as those kept for other types of surgical procedures—even the actual number of abortions performed annually is not known. However, if only 5 percent of the estimated twenty million women who have been aborted since 1973 experienced PAS, we are talking about a million women.

Where does one get training for PAS counseling?

Unfortunately, there are few places available and few professionals currently qualified to provide such training. Hopefully, as the effects of PAS become more widely known, professional schools will include this in their curriculum. Meanwhile, most techniques used to treat post-traumatic stress disorder can be adapted to treat PAS.

What do I do if a patient says, "I've dealt with the abortion"?

If she can talk freely about the abortion and not display denial or an inappropriate emotional reaction, you can assume she has dealt with the abortion. If not, then follow the treatment guidelines given in this book.

Don't pro-life materials help trigger PAS?

No. Guilt is "issue specific" and based on our own self evaluation of our past behavior measured against our own values. It can't be artificially induced.

Isn't PAS caused by prior problems?

No. PAS is directly related to the abortion and the abortion experience itself. Of course, prior problems may intensify or exaggerate PAS.

I know someone who has had an abortion and is having problems, but she doesn't know that I know. How can I help?

Unless you are her counselor, you should not confront her. If she wants you to know, she'll tell you. If and when that time comes, you should be supportive and ready to respond with understanding, compassion and possible referral for professional help. (You might give her a copy of this book.)

I can see where PAS may occur with a saline abortion, but why would it develop with a less traumatic vacuum aspiration?

In many cases, vacuum aspiration isn't as painless as it is said to be. Besides pain is only one of the stressors possibly leading to PAS. The reality of loss is traumatic in and of itself.

What are factors that increase the risk of developing postabortion syndrome?

Age: younger women are more likely to develop PAS.
Type of Procedure: the more traumatic, the more likely.
Multiple abortions: likelihood increases with repetition.
Prior history: preexisting emotional and psychological problems.

Who can help determine if a woman is suffering from PAS?

Diagnosis should be done by a professional with specific knowledge regarding the diagnosis and treatment of PAS. However, anyone who has been aborted and suffers from PAS-like symptoms should seek professional care.

What kind of self-help is available?

Women Exploited by Abortion (WEBA), Open ARMs, Abortion Victims of America (AVA) and a variety of other local or regional self-help groups can generally be found through church groups and mental health and social service organizations.

Appendix E

Forms

The questionnaires on the following pages may be reproduced and used by counselors in diagnosing and treating PAS. Their use is detailed in chapters 6 and 7 of this book.

Preinterview Written Abortion History

(to be filled out by patient as part of routine precounseling questionnaire.)

1. Have you ever had an abortion? ____ yes ____ no
2. If yes, what type? ____ vacuum aspiration ____ saline ____D&C ____ other (if other, specify type) _____
3. Where did the abortion take place? ____ doctor's office ____ hospital ____ abortion clinic ____ other (specify)_____
4. How many abortions have you had? ____ one ____ two ____ three ____ other
5. Which abortion did you just describe? _____
6. Date(s) of abortion(s):
   _____ month _____ date _____ year
   _____ month _____ date _____ year
   _____ month _____ date _____ year
   _____ month _____ date _____ year
7. In the most recent procedure:
   Did you remain hospitalized? _____ If yes, how long? _____
   Was there postabortion bleeding? ____ yes ____ no
   Did you pass anything like a blood clot after the abortion?
   ____ yes ____ no
   Have you had cramps beyond the usual menstrual cramps since the abortion? ____ yes ____ no
   Did the abortion cause other medical problems? ____ yes ____ no

Preabortion History Form

(given orally only to women diagnosed with PAS)

1. Who came with you to the facility?

2. What kind of day was it?

3. How did you get to the clinic?

4. What conversations did you have on the way to the clinic?

5. What emotions were you feeling on the way to the clinic?

6. What did the building look like?

7. Where did you park?

8. What happened prior to the abortion?

9. Did you see a counselor? _____ yes _____ no

10. Did you see a film or look at other informational materials?
    ___yes ___ no.
    If "yes," what did you see?

11. Did the counselor discuss any alternatives to abortion or ask if
    you were certain this was what you wanted? _____ yes ____ no

12. What emotions did you have while in the clinic prior to the abortion?

13. What did the waiting room look like?

14. Where did your husband/boyfriend/friend/family member
    wait?

15. Who else was in the waiting room?

16. What were the people in the waiting room feeling?

17. What did you feel about the staff that spoke with you?

18. Who paid for the abortion?

19. How was the bill paid?

Abortion History Form

(given orally only to women diagnosed with PAS)

1. What did the dressing room look like?

2. Was there a support person with you? ____ yes ____ no
    If "yes," was the support person a nurse? ____ yes ____ no

3. What did the room where the abortion took place look like?

4. Did this room have a particular smell? ____ yes ____ no
    If "yes," where else have you smelled this smell?

5. How many people were in the room?

6. Were your legs put in stirrups?

7. Were you draped with sheets? ____ yes ____ no

8. Was there physical pain:
    A. During the insertion of the instruments into your body?
    ____ yes ____ no
    B. During the procedure itself? ____ yes ____ no
    C. After the procedure? ____ yes ____ no

9. Were you given any drugs prior to the procedure?
    ____ yes ____ no
    If "yes," what drugs were you given?
    A. general anesthetic? ____ yes ____ no
    B. local anesthetic? ____ yes ____ no
    C. other? _____ (specify if known)

10. Could you see the machine? ____ yes ____ no

11. While you were lying on the table, what could you see?

12. While the procedure was going on, where was the nursing staff in the room?

13. What were you thinking while the procedure was going on?

14. What did the doctor look like?

15. Did the doctor speak to you? _____ yes _____ no
    If "yes," what did he or she say?

16. Did you see any of the products of the abortion? _____ yes _____ no
    A. If "yes," did the staff show them to you? _____ yes _____ no
    B. If "no," how did you see them?
    C. What did the products look like?

17. What did the staff do with the products of the abortion?

18. What was the general emotional tone of the abortion room?

19. What did you feel while you were lying there?

20. Did you have tears during the procedure? _____ yes _____ no
    If "yes," why were you crying?

21. Did you want to stop the procedure? _____ yes _____ no
    If "yes," why did you want to stop the procedure?

22. Did you try and stop the procedure? _____ yes _____ no
    If "yes," what was the staff's response?

23. What did you say to yourself but not to others while you were on the table?

24. What did you notice about yourself physically immediately after the abortion?

25. What did the recovery room look like?

26. What did they give you in the recovery room?

27. How long were you in the recovery room?

28. Was anyone else in the recovery room? _____ yes _____ no
    If "yes," what did that person or persons look like?

29. What did you say to yourself but not to others in the recovery room?

30. What feelings have you had since that you didn't have or couldn't express then?

31. When did your husband/boyfriend/friend next see you after the abortion?

32. What do you remember about the ride home?

33. What were the next few days like?

34. Did you keep the abortion a secret? If so, how did you keep it a secret from
    A. spouse or boyfriend

    B. family

    C. friends

    D. co-workers

    E. people at church

    F. others

Postabortion History Form

(given orally only to women diagnosed with PAS)

1. Have you had any pelvic or stomach pain? ____ yes ____ no

2. What is *your word* for what was aborted? ____ POC ____ fetus
   ____ baby ____ other (specify: _____)

3. Have you talked with the baby in your mind? ____ yes ____ no
   If "yes," what did you say?

4. Have you ever experienced the baby's presence? ____ yes ____ no
   If "yes," explain.

5. Does the baby have a sex? ____ yes ____ no
   If "yes," what sex is the baby?

6. Has the baby a visual appearance when you think about
   him/her? ____ yes ____ no
   If "yes," what does he/she look like?

7. Have you given the baby an age? ____ yes ____ no
   If "yes," what age?

8. Did the baby feel pain during the abortion? ____ yes ____ no
   If "yes," explain.

9. Where is the baby now?

10. Did you grieve over the loss of the baby? ____ yes ____ no

11. Have you had other children since the abortion? ____ yes ____ no
    If "yes," how many?

12. Have you had a miscarriage since the abortion? ____ yes ____ no
    If "yes," how many?

13. Are you still with the biological father of the aborted baby/POC?
    ____ yes ____ no

14. Do you still think about the abortion? ____ yes ____ no
    If "yes," how often?

15. Do certain sights or sounds remind you of the abortion?
    ____ yes____ no
    If "yes," describe them.

16. Have you ever had dreams about the abortion? ____ yes ____ no
    If "yes," describe them.

17. Have you ever had dreams about the aborted baby/POC (use her word)? ____ yes ____ no
    If "yes," describe them.

18. Where do you think the baby/POC (use her word) is now?

19. Do you feel sad or depressed on the anniversary date of the abortion? ____ yes ____ no
    If "yes," describe your feelings.

20. Do you have a difficult time bonding with babies or young children? ____ yes ____ no

21. Does the media coverage of the abortion issue affect you?
    ____ yes ____ n
    If "yes," in what way does it affect you?

22. Were your relationships changed as a result of the abortion?
    ____ yes ____ no
    If "yes" describe how your relationship was changed with
    A. spouse or boyfriend

    B. family

    C. friends

    D. co-workers

    E. people at church

    F. others

23. Were other areas of your life changed as a result? ____ yes ____ no
    If "yes," describe how.
    A. social

B. spiritual

C. sexual

D. emotional

E. physical (problems)

24. Did you make any attempts to remedy the problem? ____ yes ____ no
    If "yes," can you give three examples?
    A.
    B.
    C.

25. Have you experienced any startle reactions? ____ yes ____ no
    If "yes," what were these like?
    A.
    B.
    C.

26. Have your values been affected by the abortion? ____ yes ____ no.
    If "yes," give three examples.
    A.
    B.
    C.

27. Has your character been affected by the abortion? ____ yes ____ no
    If "yes," how has it affected your
    A. trust
    B. honesty
    C. openness
    D. caring
    E. integrity
    F. other

28. Describe where the baby/product of conception is at this time.

29. Describe ten times when your feelings were saying one thing and
    your behavior was saying another in regards to the abortion
    decision, the abortion, and afterward.
    1.
    2.

3.
4.
5.
6.
7.
8.
9.
10.

30. Detail five things you are going to do in the future in order not to let yourself fall back emotionally or mentally.
    1.
    2.
    3.
    4.
    5.

Notes

Preface

1. In the counseling profession, it is common to use the term *aborted women* rather than the more cumbersome *women who have had abortions.*

Chapter 1

1. Diagnostic and Statistical Manual of Mental Disorders.
2. According to the Surgeon General's final draft report, "Medical and Psychological Effects of Abortion on Women" (22 March 1989), "The American Psychiatric Association has identified abortion as a 'psychosocial stressor.' Some clinicians and researchers consider abortion a psychosocial stressor capable of causing what they call postabortion syndrome, which they consider a form of post-traumatic stress disorder." Hereafter, references to this report will refer to it as the "Surgeon General's report on abortion."
3. "Two well-known outcomes are discussed in the abortion debates. At one end of the continuum are women who have had abortions and who state that the health and psychological effects have been beneficial. At the other end are those women who have had abortions and who state that the operation has left them grieving for their lost infant and has caused them anxiety, depression, and guilt. *For some women these feelings may not be triggered until years after the event. However, there is a third group about which little is said and who say little. Those are the women who have had an abortion but who, for whatever reason, deny that they have done so. Their feelings remain private and unknown.*" Surgeon General's report on abortion (emphasis added).
4. Age may also have been a contributing factor in post-Vietnam stress disorder. In World War II, the average age of an American soldier was twenty-five or twenty-six. In Vietnam, it was nineteen. Nineteen-year-olds have a less efficient coping mechanism than do twenty-six-year-olds. Of course, the political situation was different too. Returning

WW II veterans were considered conquering heroes, welcomed with brass bands and parades—quite differently from the way returning Vietnam vets were greeted.

5. Women Exploited by Abortion (WEBA) does offer a national forum and offers support for aborted women. Also, Abortion Victims of America (AVA) is a part of the National Right to Life organization and offers support. However, since these groups are closely allied with the pro-life movement, they have been largely ignored by pro-choice advocates and by many clinicians who shun "political involvement."

Chapter 2

1. All names and identifying details are changed to protect the privacy of actual patients. Histories are on file.

Chapter 5

1. According to the Surgeon General's report on abortion, "No comprehensive system exists for collecting data on abortion in the United States. The Centers for Disease Control (CDC) operates an abortion surveillance program that gathers information from approximately forty state health departments and from individual hospitals and clinics within the ten remaining states. The Alan Guttmacher Institute (AGI) also publishes abortion statistics. Their findings supplement the CDC data with information obtained *from service providers who do not report to state health departments*. The AGI statistics generally report 15 to 20 percent more abortions than do the CDC's findings (emphasis added)."

2. According to the Surgeon General's report on abortion, 81 percent of abortions are performed on single women and 50 percent of all teen pregnancies end in abortion.

3. If, for example, the woman is told the item removed is merely a "mass of cells" and she happens to catch a glimpse of something being removed that looks different or later sees the *LIFE* magazine interuterine photographs, she may understandably feel she was misinformed.

4. True counseling has the *client's best interest* at heart. A woman suffering from PAS frequently feels the counselor at the abortion clinic was more interested in "making a sale" than in providing true counseling. After all, she wonders, could the counselor at the clinic have kept her job if she'd told me the down side of abortion? Whether or not there is any basis in fact for these feelings, in today's litigious society, they are potentially dangerous to the abortion industry.

Chapter 7

1. The Surgeon General's report on abortion says, "The resolution of postabortion syndrome for men and women requires the individual to acknowledge what an abortion is, that he or she has participated in a death experience, that a loss has occurred, and that grieving and forgiveness are necessary."

Appendix A

1. From the American Psychiatric Association's Diagnostic and Statistical Manual of Mental Disorders (Third Edition-Revised.)

Appendix B

1. Based on APA guidelines for post-traumatic stress disorder (see Appendix A) and those developed by Vincent Rue.

2. The Surgeon General's report on Abortion simplifies the symptoms with these words: "As previously noted, this condition has been characterized as postabortion syndrome. The symptoms include (1) exposure to the violence of intentionally destroying one's unborn child; (2) uncontrolled and involuntary negative reexperiencing of the abortion death; (3) attempts to avoid or deny abortion pain or grief, which can result in reduced responsiveness toward one's environment; and (4) experiencing associated symptoms, including sleep disorders, depression, secondary substance abuse, intense hostility, and guilt about surviving. The course of this disorder may be acute (30 days or less), or chronic (6 months or longer), or may be delayed, occurring 5-10 years or more after the operation."

Appendix C

1. Based on the Surgeon General's report on abortion.

2. Wherever times are used, they are approximate. Sometimes the aborted woman may not know or may not be honest about the time of conception.